Creating a Self-Directed Learning Environment

Dedicated to my wife,
Jaclyn Mullen,
for taking me off the grid
and far into the forest
so I could finish my book.

Creating a Self-Directed Learning Environment

Standards-Based and Social-Emotional Learning

By Greg Mullen

FOR INFORMATION:

Corwin

A SAGE Company

2455 Teller Road

Thousand Oaks, California 91320

(800) 233-9936

www.corwin.com

SAGE Publications Ltd.

1 Oliver's Yard

55 City Road

London EC1Y 1SP

United Kingdom

SAGE Publications India Pvt. Ltd.

B 1/I 1 Mohan Cooperative Industrial Area

Mathura Road, New Delhi 110 044

India

SAGE Publications Asia-Pacific Pte. Ltd.

18 Cross Street #10-10/11/12

China Square Central

Singapore 048423

Program Director: Jessica Allan

Content Development Editor: Lucas Schleicher

Senior Editorial Assistant: Mia Rodriguez

Production Editor: Tori Mirsadjadi

Copy Editor: Tammy Giesmann

Typesetter: C&M Digitals (P) Ltd.

Proofreader: Susan Schon

Indexer: Mary Mortensen

Cover Designer: Candice Harman

Marketing Manager: Deena Meyer

Printed in the United States of America

ISBN 978-1-5443-8424-5

This book is printed on acid-free paper.

SUSTAINABLE FORESTRY INITIATIVE
Certified Chain of Custody
Promoting Sustainable Forestry
www.sfiprogram.org
SFI-01268
SFI label applies to text stock

19 20 21 22 23 10 9 8 7 6 5 4 3 2 1

Contents

Acknowledgments

AUTHOR'S ACKNOWLEDGMENTS

This book is a product of more than a decade of research and experience pushing the boundaries of the status quo in education. My role as a teacher's assistant more than a decade ago at an affluent school in West L.A. was my first look at traditionalism in education from the other side of the teacher's desk. A year later, my role as a teacher credential candidate at the Teacher Education Department at CSU, Dominguez Hills, introduced me to mentors James Cantor PhD and master teacher Jeremy Munson who provided the support and practical guidance for an innovative spirit within a traditional school system. My time at Lindsay Unified School District, under the guidance of the Learning Director and my professional mentor Gina Wise and collaborative support of colleagues Steven Miller and Ycxia Padron, introduced me to concepts of performance-based education and took me further into improving the status quo, promoting innovative spirit, and challenging traditionalism in education. The years that followed introduced a number of excellent educators for whom I am forever thankful, in addition to the support of friends and family, including: Adam Corcoran, Alma Jongewaard, Angela Kappner, Brian Post, and the late Dr. Donna Post, Jordan Vargas, Leila Turner, Meg Bristow, Nicholas Zagorin, Sabrina Lozano, Sarah Limongelli, Sonya Brannan, Susan Botana—their openness and willingness to listen and philosophize with me bolstered that innovative spirit, spurring my desire to further research and develop the philosophy and framework detailed in this book.

When I completed my first draft, I felt it was important to acknowledge the insightful initial feedback by education specialist Stephanie Davis EdM, innovative educator Gerry Piccini, and the creative literary mind of Sue Nelson. I especially wish to acknowledge Ken O'Connor and Matt Townsley for their expertise and tutelage of so many educators shifting to a standards-based approach. I also wish to thank the team at Corwin for their care of this book in support of a standards-based social-emotional approach to self-directed learning.

Finally, to my students, I wish to share a letter I wrote after a particularly powerful school year that has since proved to be true for every class of self-directed learners whom I've had the pleasure of teaching:

> Today was my last day of teaching . . . All day, I was restating the following thoughts that they've heard a million times before from me—the ideas I just don't want them to forget . . .
>
> Think—as well as do. Challenge each other to be better and you, as well as those around you, will grow. Keep your sights on what you want most. Compare yourself only to that which you want to become. It will not be easy, but if you train yourself to know what it is to work hard, it will not feel so impossible. I know you can, I've seen you do it, and every day when you wake up, know that somebody believes you can. The poetry readings, debates, presentations, event planning, all began with the largest obstacle—standing up and deciding to go through with it. These were all tasks you chose to participate in; I never marked anybody down for deciding not to stand up and participate. Yet nearly every single one of you took part in many, if not all, of these tasks. Some of you stumbled, and received encouragement from your peers, and each one of you agreed that the hardest part was standing up. To those that chose not to stand up: you will decide one day to stand, and when you do, you will do so when you're ready and be that much more prepared for what is coming. Talk to people. Talk to each other, talk to your teachers, talk to your family, share your ideas and support others who share theirs. If you've learned nothing else (I hope not!), please remember that we share this classroom, this school, this community, this land, and you will someday be in charge of it. Think. Challenge. Grow. and Have a Good Summer!

—Greg Mullen

PUBLISHER'S ACKNOWLEDGMENTS

Corwin gratefully acknowledges the contributions of the following reviewers:

Jessica Baldwin
Teacher
Toombs County High School
Lyons, GA

Charla Buford Bunker
Literacy Specialist
Great Falls High School
Great Falls, MT

Deb Bible
Educational Consultant
DeKalb Regional Office of Education
DeKalb, IL

Christine Clement
Instructional Coach
Mandeville Middle School
Mandeville, LA

Lisa Graham
Director, Early Childhood
    Education
Douglas County School District
Lone Tree, CO

Ashley LaCroix
Technology Integrator
Wiscasset Elementary School
Wiscasset, ME

Meghan Schofield
Third Grade Teacher
Wiscasset Elementary School
Wiscasset, ME

About the Author

Author Photo Credit: *A&C Photography*
www.AdamAndClaudiaPhotography.com/

Greg Mullen is a credentialed educator who has spent the past few years developing an approach toward standards-based education through a lens of social-emotional learning. Inspired by his years as a classroom teacher in California public, private, and charter schools, his focus now is helping schools, teachers, and families troubleshoot obstacles in personalizing education. He enjoys spending his spare time researching across academic disciplines and occasionally performing as a rock musician. Having released his first book, *Creating a Self-Directed Learning Environment*, he continues to write and speak on topics of personalizing education across the country. Learn more about his work at www.ExploringTheCore.com

Introduction

EXPLORING THE CORE

Exploring is an extremely difficult task, especially when time is not an infinite resource. It requires patience, a curious spirit, and a willingness to be wrong at times. Most important, exploring requires a question or a topic to be considered. Exploring will inevitably result in findings related to the question or topic that spur other questions or topics that go well beyond what was being explored in the first place.

My exploration began with a fairly general topic: to understand the Common Core State Standards. I began with the math standards and quickly discovered patterns of specific skill development in and across grade levels. Some math concepts such as place value are rooted in nearly all grade levels while other concepts such as fractions start at the third-grade level and stop at the end of the fifth-grade level. This insight to skill development helped me to see how concepts such as place value develop as early as kindergarten and on through upper-elementary and middle school math skills. This also helped me to see how the concept of place value supported those skills that seemed to develop quite quickly over a shorter period of time such as fractions in grades three through five. It seemed to me that each standard had been crafted to account for how a skill develops both in and across grade levels. When I dove into the Common Core State Standards for English Language Arts, I saw similar and more explicit skill development that allowed me to identify the expected understanding implied across grade-level standards. Exploring these ideas allowed me to identify how academic gaps can form leaving both teacher and student in a lurch if a student did not master a particular grade-level skill.

Because I was exploring and open to discovery, I compared my findings with the Common Core State Standards to other states' standards. It was very cool to see how standards across states align not by grade level specifically but by skill development. Certain aspects of a skill's development occur in a particular order no matter what state standards I explored. The biggest difference was the differences in how quickly different skills developed across grade levels. The way standards were phrased and organized was also a major difference but it began to seem as though the *intent* of the standards and how they developed skills across grade levels was consistent across states.

This initial exploration evolved into an analysis of implementing grading practices, defining proficiency, and utilizing assessments. I began to feel that these academic standards were intentionally written to guide educators through these other aspects. Skills are defined in these standards and aligned by grade level, but it became clear to me that each skill is not dependent on the grade level as a measure of time but as a measure of individual skill development.

As I continued to explore these deeper-rooted inquiries into the implementation of academic standards, I found myself exploring a related area of education—social and emotional learning. This extension of my original exploration was the result of conversations regarding student obstacles that were not rooted in the academic standards but in classroom management and student motivation. The more I explored, the more I began to realize the many correlations between social and emotional learning and academic achievement.

This exploration eventually led me to consider both the causal and correlative relationships between cognitive, psychosocial, and social-emotional development with regard to academic progress. I came to believe that development in one of these areas will struggle when development in other areas also struggle. I would ask colleagues the following hypothetical question in order to spark discussion: "If a child was raised by animals without any human social or emotional upbringing, would the child develop the cognitive brain functions to be a fully functioning human adult?" This would typically ignite conversation and fractalize out to include such topics as culture, environment, and related interests in child development, resulting in healthy discussion but without conclusive consensus.

Today, my exploration now involves the connections between academic, social-emotional, and human development, and has created a unique perspective that I now hold very dear. It is a perspective that requires an awareness of interconnectivity of these exclusive areas of study. I now use three conjoining circles to represent these three areas and how they can be overlapped, combined, to create new (secondary) concepts. At the center of these three circles is the core of my exploration. This core is an idea that looks at the whole person and an idea that I hope will spark value in others exploring their own self, others around them, as well as their communities both small and large.

I am thankful for the freedom of my exploration, unrestrained and interdisciplinary, that allowed me to connect with various professionals in areas of academic, social-emotional, and cognitive development. The value of my findings, from my own perspective as an educator, has been incredibly helpful to my own development and I hope others will continue exploring these connections and further their own findings.

It is important to me that every person be allowed their own personal and professional perspectives and to determine value of any exploratory findings as they relate to their needs. Exploring has been, and will continue to be, a privilege and I thank my colleagues, friends, family, and you, the reader, for taking the time to consider the core of this exploration toward creating a self-directed learning environment.

WHEN EVERYTHING WAS PERFECT

In the year 2011, I began my first year of full-time teaching in Lindsay, California. I had a multiple-subject credential and had been a substitute teacher for about a year in Los Angeles. The Los Angeles Unified School District had reacted to a national recession with a hiring freeze so teaching jobs were few and far apart. When I was finally hired as a seventh-grade teacher, I was hesitant to pick up and move to central California because it meant moving away from my soon-to-be wife who had a fruitful career in Los Angeles. Excited to start a career of my own, I had less than a month before the school year started and couldn't wait to set up my classroom and begin planning for the school year.

Some details I evidently overlooked, but nonetheless would not have deterred my decision, involved the depth of change the Lindsay Unified School District had just undergone. The district had decided to adopt *performance-based education* at a time when California had only just adopted the Common Core State Standards and had not developed materials or assessment tools for the new standards. That same summer, they had disbanded their middle school and turned the K–5 school sites into K–8 school sites; such was my role as a seventh-grade multiple-subject teacher. Another detail I wouldn't understand until it happened was the multi-age nature of a performance-based system that had advanced sixth-, at-level seventh-, and remedial eighth-grade students all mixed together in different subjects depending on their ability.

The seventh-grade students on that first day of school had then seen up to eight years of traditional classroom teaching and, so far, were clearly unimpressed. The student ability levels were so wide ranging that my attempts to foster a traditional style of teaching were causing traditional behavior problems to persist. The low-achieving students were not interested in any lessons, classwork, homework, independent work, group work, or any work that involved anything they didn't already know how to do. The high-achieving students were bored at the middle-of-the-road lessons and assignments and my knowledge of grade-level standards were such that offering advanced or otherwise forward-thinking tasks and projects for all the seventh-grade standards had been incredibly overwhelming. This left all students looking to me, their teacher, for something a lot of teachers were untrained and unexperienced in providing that first year—individualized learning opportunities. It took time to begin implementing this concept of allowing learners to take ownership of their own learning and only tracking their progress with the standards or groups of standards as individual students progressed.

ıfter two productive and memorable years with this performance-based model, another year as a substitute teacher in Los Angeles, and a year as a middle school teacher for a charter school in North Hollywood, I took the plunge to spend a year away from the classroom, fully exploring academic standards. That year of exploration resulted in the creation of mobile apps that aligned standards such that users could swipe across grade levels to see how skills develop. My hope was that students and parents would be empowered to discuss with teachers how to close gaps in learning by identifying in which grade levels certain skills had become difficult for that student. That idea did not resonate with the general public, but I was hired again the following year as a third-grade classroom teacher.

I now consider Standards-Based Grading (SBG) to be a big part of my classroom by this point and I now spend more of my time developing individual responsibility, self-efficacy, goal-setting, empathetic reasoning, and community. Some days my academic lesson plan would be dismissed completely in order for my students to explore a standard that they were interested in learning and track development of that learning. My knowledge of the standards allows me to quickly determine which standards students are working on and identify targets for tracking growth. Instruction is adjusted based on social-emotional needs while also adjusting to meet proficiency levels for students. This creates a freedom in my classroom that allows both me and my students to coexist in what I call a self-directed learning environment. It is in these moments, when all three aspects of my exploration overlap in the classroom, that freedom and exploration toward learning is the focus and the role of teacher and student become transparent and cooperative—it is in these moments when everything is perfect.

It is important to note that in these moments when everything is perfect, there are aspects that require patience and leniency toward student learning. Lesson planning for individual student needs can become overwhelming at first, especially when traditional lesson planning may not fully support such an approach. Standards-based assessments and grading may not align with school-wide demands of time-based reporting of student proficiency. More than anything else, it can become difficult communicating the importance of growth over proficiency and a student's developing ability to be self-directed, especially when end-of-year reporting only shows proficiency of grade-level academic standards.

Now consider in that same learning environment, when everything is perfect, students are conscious of their freedom to work on the standards they know they need to master to be fully prepared for the next grade level— students are exercising their ability to be self-directed learners. Obedience and accountability in this environment are self-regulated. Students know, academically, what they have mastered as much as what they haven't mastered for their grade level. Students learn, emotionally, to motivate themselves through ongoing collaborative problem solving. Students know which strategies support which academic skills and cooperate with others to practice strategies not yet mastered.

When everything is perfect, my responsibilities as a teacher overlap with the responsibilities of my learners. My role is less about instructing the academic material and more about monitoring and supporting, guiding and encouraging, and suggesting pathways that support productive strategies for individual students to overcome their obstacles. When everything is perfect, I support individual student learning of academic skills through a social-emotional lens, considering the appropriate development of each student. For me as the classroom teacher, it is the human that I am teaching, not the subject.

PERFECT CIRCLES HAVE NO BEGINNING

The following is a loose metaphor to explain a challenging idea.

When I look at a perfect circle drawn on a page, the infinite number of points on a circle are fluidly inked to overlap and make it look as though there is no beginning. However, there clearly was a start to that perfect circle and it is only due to illusion that I would think otherwise. Perfect circles I see were typically created mechanically, by an electronically programmed printer. I have seen circles created by human hands that seem perfect but are wrought with insignificant imperfections.

Every year, teachers draw themselves a new circle as they prepare for a new school year. They think about their circle over the summer and draw it the weeks before school begins. The drawing of this circle involves a lot of hustle and bustle amongst teachers to prepare their classroom environments, plan first month activities, backward plan academic goals, set up grading systems, and many other preparatory responsibilities. For the newest teachers, this process can be daunting and overwhelming, and they collaborate with their colleagues to seek out the routines they feel might fit their personality and instructional needs. As years pass, these responsibilities become prioritized with a sense of balance as they become increasingly well-versed in various aspects of preparing for a new school year, carrying with them a bag of tricks and resources so that we are as prepared for the new school year as we know we must be.

While it can seem to new teachers that the veteran teacher unpacks their classroom from a ready-made kit, it is irrational to think that there was no beginning to their preparing for the new school year. To a new teacher, it may seem that an intuition is at work, that these teachers just "have it all together." It is this idea of intuition and its development through intention where I find value in this metaphor of a perfect circle.

Imagine drawing a circle. Your page is blank—it is your first circle. You want it to be perfect. You've been trained in how to draw a circle and you have every intention of making your circle perfect. As you draw your circle, you find that some parts of the circle are straighter than others, there's a spot of extra ink at one point, and you have had to correct your circle to meet your original starting point. It almost seems like you were spiraling away from where you had begun and corrected it.

Before you begin judging your circle, consider how a spiral is drawn. A spiral is not a circle. It expands outward with each revolution. Over time, however, with thoughtful intent, each revolution may follow itself outward and begin to feel as if a circle is being drawn with each revolution. You can control the speed and path of each revolution to follow the path of previous revolutions so closely as to overlap in places. With time, over several revolutions, you begin to see the perfection of your circle as the best of past revolutions are overlapped by newer revolutions until almost all points of your tightly controlled spiral begins to resemble a circle that; to others, may be called artistic, intuitive, perfect.

For me, as a new school year approaches, I see that I no longer have a blank page to draw a new circle. I see my overlapping circles. I see the gaps between them, the imperfections of each one, and look to this next revolution as an opportunity to follow the best of prior circles and adjust to fill in the gaps— all the while knowing this next revolution will have its own imperfections. Yet, at the start of each school year, I begin a new circle and both learn from, and strengthen, past circles. Perfect circles, for me as a teacher, have no beginning because I spiral my circles to strengthen each passing revolution to create a bold resemblance of a perfect circle.

There are three circles that I have been strengthening with intention, each school year strengthening the last. The following chapters detail my own exploration and practice of the following three concepts: Standards-Based Grading, Social and Emotional Learning, and Human Development. It is my intention, throughout the chapters in this book, to address how all three concepts can overlap and provide insight into larger concepts of Self-Directed Learning as well as Behavioral and Academic Inclusion and Intervention. When all three circles overlap, what is created is the core of my philosophy and framework toward education.

PART 1

Primary Concepts

The three primary concepts in this section are three exclusive components that are critical to creating a healthy, self-directed learning environment. Each concept is explored separately from my perspective as a classroom teacher addressing social-emotional learning through the vehicle of standards-based grading according to the human development needs of my students.

The first primary concept is an approach called Standards-Based Grading (SBG). It creates a classroom instructional environment of transparency and accountability for tracking academic growth.

The second primary concept is an approach to Social-Emotional Learning (SEL). It addresses behavior expectations through an awareness of scope that provides context for reasonable systems of behavior management.

The third primary concept is an approach to cognitive and psychosocial human development. It serves to understand the shared roles of general and special education and promote unity in shared responsibilities toward educating all students.

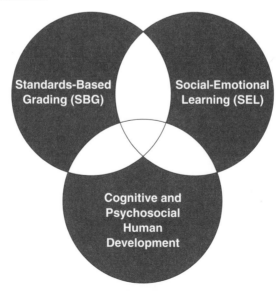

CHAPTER 1

Standards-Based Grading

There have been many books published on the topic of standards-based grading. This chapter is not intended to replace or revise the practices of those published works. My intention for this chapter on standards-based grading is to provide insight into the purpose and potential for positive uses of a standards-based grading approach. It has become part of my philosophy that standards-based grading is a critical first step to creating a self-directed learning environment. Each section of this chapter covers an aspect of standards-based grading that I feel is important to understand and internalize so as to gain a better sense of why a teacher would want to implement this first concept.

The traditional teacher that is not fully standards based will likely have some practices and beliefs that may need to wholly change. Yet, the value of a standards-based classroom will increase with this transition of the teacher's perspective. The biggest takeaways for a self-directed learning environment begin to appear as the students internalize that same shift in their own perspective toward expectations, responsibilities, and the acceptance of their own capacity as a self-directed student.

TEACHER MASTERY OF STANDARDS

Standards-Based Grading begins with an analysis of academic standards for the grade level assigned to be taught. It is important to analyze where each standard is coming from in its development from prior years. It is as important to also know where each standard is heading in its development in later years. This analysis provides several beneficial allowances.

First, this allows the dissection of standards of which students will expect their teacher to have insight and mastery. It is not enough to know what the standard expects of the student but how the student can master each standard in various ways. This takes time on the part of the teacher to fully understand the myriad of possible tasks and strategies that can develop a skill.

This also allows each standard to align with prior grade-level standards and provide insight into academic strategies that may have been taught to students in prior years. Past strategies may be useful at the grade level they were taught but may require adjustment to account for an increase in complexity to the current expected academic outcome. By considering the development of a skill according to the standards across grade levels, strategies may be used as scaffolds that give students more ownership of approaching problem solving in a way that will benefit them in later grade levels. This requires that both the teacher and the student communicate not only the strategy but *the value and awareness of purpose* for a strategy with respect to a given skill's development.

Most important, the teacher's mastery of standards will eventually provide students the freedom to move on or go back to any grade-level standard and have the confidence that instructional guidance for any skill will be available to them from the teacher or other available resources. This will become a major component in developing a self-directed learning environment.

STANDARDS AND GRADING

Determining which grading practice is appropriate for each standard is a process in and of itself. This determination of grading practice connects to how teachers break down tasks that develop the mastery of grade-level standards.

Percentage-Based Grading

There are a number of common grading practices to consider when grading different standards. The most prevalent practice is the percentage-based grading practice. Any approach that relies on a calculation of *student work correct* over a total amount of *correct work possible* can be considered a percentage-based grading practice.

For example, if an assessment has seven questions and the student correctly answers four of them, regardless of what the questions entail, the result can be communicated as a score of four out of seven (57 percent). This becomes a serious concern when the assessment is not designed such that missing any three of those seven questions would validate a *failing* score.

A more reasonable use of this grading practice might involve large quantities of work such as fluency speed tests for math facts or spelling (presuming that such tasks have been deemed appropriate for assessing proficiency). However, keep in mind that if an assessment has twenty math facts to be completed within a particular amount of time, a student who correctly answers more than ten (50 percent) but less than fifteen (75 percent) may consider themselves failing that particular standard. Because of these quick and convenient uses of percentage-based scoring, it is easily the most misused and miscommunicated form of grading.

My own experience with percentage-based grading is that students become obsessed with bringing up their percentage score by ignoring the content they didn't master and seeking to complete other *extra* assignments or projects unrelated to standards not mastered. I also find difficulty using a single percentage score to communicate results of an assessment that may contain more than one skill or standard.

Pass-Fail Grading

Another common grading practice is the pass-fail method. This is common for basic skills and standards that have little to no gray area of process or concept. Memorizing a fact for recall is a low-level cognitive task for which I may grade as a *pass* or *not pass*. I may use this when students are learning phonics or describing in one sentence a main idea of a passage. Lower elementary has many standards at this basic recall level but, as students reach higher grade levels, they may see less of this grading method as the cognitive complexity of tasks increase. Skills or standards that build on sections of a procedure or concept may need a grading method that accounts for these higher-levels of cognitive complexity and rigor.

Rubric Grading

Another common grading practice is the rubric. This practice becomes useful as the cognitive complexity of tasks increase. Points-based rubrics may be used to communicate objective expectations of growth in student learning with any number of points to be considered for grading purposes, depending on the skill or standard.

Today, I see four-point rubrics being used often but have seen up to six-point rubrics applied to specific tasks. Rubrics for writing often have several sets of expectations separated into a multi-point rubric to account for grammar, content, voice, and other such writing-related skills. I've also seen five-point rubrics used for projects that have five distinct components that must be completed for full credit. It is important to recognize how easy it is to use a rubric as a point-counting system that does not specifically and objectively reflect student learning according to the standard being addressed. Point-based rubrics can easily become a means of calculating points earned over total points possible—which then becomes a percentage-based grade.

I often have students who will receive two out of four points on a rubric and reinterpret that as 50 percent and tell other students that they have *failed*. These students have learned to equate their learning with a percentage and associate that percentage with their proficiency of a skill or standard. This goes against the intended beliefs of a standards-based grading system that promotes high-quality feedback for students to interpret as progress toward mastery. Rubric grading will more often be used with a multi-standard task that, when giving feedback on each rubric item, may seem like more work but can be time-saving in the long run.

Letter Grades

Traditionally, this is the most popular form of grading. Letter grades are essentially a glorified percentage-based grading system that organizes ranges of percentage scores and simplifies each range of percentage scores to assigned letters such as A, B, C, D, and F.

The simplicity in writing a single letter to represent student learning has become a common expectation for teachers and parents. It seems receiving a letter grade represents a percentage score within a percentage range to communicate content mastery. As a student growing up, I never felt that my own mastery of a skill was up to me and that the letter grade I received meant only what the teacher told me I had learned. When I received a 'C' on an assignment or report card, I only knew it was *enough to pass*. I saw other students who received a 'B' as having learned more than me but less than those that received an 'A'. At no point was it made clear to me what those letters meant beyond my own interpretation of learning or not learning. Today, I see students going through this same percentage-based letter grade system and realize that they, like me, have little to no idea what those letter grades mean with regard to their own learning.

Transfer of Scales

The particular grading scales chosen by a teacher for marking individual assignments and assessments will likely involve multiple grading scales. Each mark must only communicate to what level of proficiency a student has or has not mastered a particular standard or skill. If a student has shown mastery of a required standard, that should be the only information used to develop a final grade. When it comes to students *almost* mastering a standard, this is discussed in more detail in the next section: Defining Proficiency.

It is critical that individual assignment scores *avoid transferring between scales*. Every grading scale is used to provide feedback on a particular task. Proficiency is set according to that task. Marks students receive communicate the level of mastery for that task and that standard. Transferring a score from one grading scale to another can confuse the level of mastery a student has acquired for a standard.

GRADING SCALES ARE NOT EQUAL			
4	A	< 100	Advanced
3	B	< 90	Proficient
2	C	< 80	Basic
1	D	< 70	Below Basic
0	F	< 60	Far Below Basic
Information does not transfer equally between them.			

At the end of a grading period, it will be the mastery of each skill or standard that will be communicated, not the averaging of pseudo-equivalent percentage scores for each assignment. Whatever grading scales are chosen, they must be specific to the task and communicate mastery appropriate for each standard.

When using any grading scale, address the specific learning task with a specific range of learning outcomes based on the specific scale for grading. The purpose for this strict adherence to the use of grading scales communicating mastery of standards is to help students learn how to describe what they have and have not learned based on the expectations of a particular skill or standard. This becomes critical in a self-directed learning environment.

DEFINING PROFICIENCY

Proficient is a word widely used but rarely defined. It is my opinion that a single definition for this word would set an extraordinarily unrealistic expectation for standards in subjects across all grade levels. It is also my opinion that the word *proficient* should be defined such that it is relevant to the skill or standard being mastered, in each subject, at each grade level. It is also my opinion that words synonymous with this term such as Mastery, Competency, "At Level", Meeting Expectations, and the like, are not to replace or reassign its purpose. To define proficiency, a standard must be referred to as it relates to the development of a skill within and across grade levels. For this approach toward defining proficiency, I prefer to use the language associated with the four levels of Webb's Depth of Knowledge, as noted in the following figure.

4 Beyond Instructional Expectations

Students creatively connect strategic reasoning and evidence of concepts and skills to materials and events beyond the intended expectations of the provided instructional goals.

(Continued)

(Continued)

> **3 Strategic Reasoning and Evidence**
>
> *Students communicate an understanding of a concept or skill that incorporates strategically organized reasoning of evidence that supports their claim of understanding.*
>
> **2 Understanding Concept/Skill**
>
> *Students communicate an appropriate depth of understanding of a concept or skill, verbally or in written form.*
>
> **1 Basic Recall/Reproduction**
>
> *Students are able to recall information and/or procedures in order to communicate understanding in various contexts.*

As will be explained in this section, a standard can be assigned as a Level 1 Proficiency standard if that standard is written such that it requires only recall or reproduction of basic information. A different standard could be written as a Level 3 Proficiency standard if it requires insightful communication of an idea through which evidence is provided as reasonable and relevant support.

The purpose of defining proficiency this way, as will be discussed in detail below, is to not only define the expected level of proficiency of individual standards but to be better prepared to communicate expectations for proficiency with students, parents, and colleagues.

The goal is to target and shift reporting language from *pass and fail* to *proficiency and growth*. It is important to recognize the level of proficiency required for each task in an assessment in order to provide relevant and meaningful feedback to students.

Before examining proficiency in various standards, I feel inclined to mention the work of Karin Hess out of Vermont, specifically her work designing a Rigor Matrix for standards.

Rigor Matrix (Task/Cognitive Complexity)

It is the work of Karin Hess that combines two popular hierarchies, Webb's Depth of Knowledge and Bloom's Taxonomy, into one system she calls her Rigor Matrix (Hess, 2018). My own approach toward defining proficiency of standards builds off of Dr. Hess's work by analyzing the text of individual standards to define what I call a Depth of Proficiency. As in Hess's Rigor Matrix, I use Bloom's Taxonomy for its verb categories and refer to these verbs in defining the *task complexity* of a standard. I also, like Hess, use Webb's Depth of Knowledge to determine the standard's context and refer to these contexts in defining the *cognitive complexity* of a standard. For example, a standard may include verbs such as translate or summarize (Bloom's

Taxonomy—Comprehension) that represent a fairly low *task complexity*. However, the context of the task may represent a higher *cognitive complexity* such as summarizing a main idea with evidence that connects character development to the theme (Webb's DOK3—Strategic Reasoning and Evidence).

When I apply this analysis of standards across grade levels, I'm able to communicate with colleagues (and students!) which skills in prior grade levels may have required tasks of lower proficiency but now require higher proficiency tasks. Not all skills develop with an increase in proficiency equal across grade levels, so defining proficiency becomes an important part of a standards-based approach.

Vertical Alignment of Proficiency

Defining the Depth of Proficiency using Bloom's and Webb's theories serves as an objective perspective toward defining proficiency specific to the standard being mastered. It is common for the lower elementary grade levels to have a higher percentage of lower task and cognitive complexity written into their standards. Upper elementary grade-level standards tend to introduce higher cognitive complexity into some of their standards. Middle and high school grade levels have a wide variety of lower and higher task and cognitive complexity written into the various grade-level standards.

It is therefore imperative to the success of all students for teachers to know how their colleagues approach proficiency in adjacent grade levels. If a prior teacher was not aware of the differences in proficiency of various standards, then there may be need to approach the start of the school year collecting information on student proficiency levels for that grade level's prerequisite standards.

For example, one of the Anchor Standards in the ELA Common Core State Standards states:

CCSS.ELA-Literacy.CCRA.R.2: Determine central ideas or themes of a text and analyze their development; summarize the key supporting details and ideas.

This means that by the time a student exits the K–12 school system, they will be able to perform tasks that meet a level of proficiency for this skill appropriate for college or career. This also means that each grade level will approach this anchor standard at a level of task and cognitive complexity appropriate to this skill's development.

For example, a second-grade classroom will be required to "*recount* stories, including fables and folktales from diverse cultures, and *determine* their central message, lesson, or moral." A third-grade classroom will "*recount* stories, including fables, folktales, and myths from diverse cultures; *determine* the central message, lesson, or moral and *explain* how it is conveyed through key details in the text." A fourth-grade classroom will "*determine* a theme of a story, drama, or poem from details in the text; *summarize* the text." A fifth-grade classroom will "*determine* a theme of a story, drama, or poem from details in the text, including how characters in a story or drama respond to challenges or how the speaker in a poem reflects upon a topic; *summarize* the text." The focus of each grade level skill is the same but increases in task and cognitive complexity across grade levels.

The following illustration shows the grade level development of this particular anchor standard from kindergarten through the eighth-grade level.

CCSS.ELA-LITERACY.CCRA.R.2:
Determine central ideas or themes of a text and analyze their development; summarize the key supporting details and ideas.

KINDERGARTEN	GRADE 1	GRADE 2
With prompting and support, retell familiar stories, including key details.	Retell stories, including key details, and demonstrate understanding of their central message or lesson.	Recount stories, including fables and folktales from diverse cultures, and determine their central message, lesson, or moral.
GRADE 3	GRADE 4	GRADE 5
Recount stories including fables, folktales, and myths from diverse cultures; determine the central message, lesson, or moral and explain how it is conveyed through key details in the text.	Determine a theme of a story, drama, or poem from details in the text, summarize the text.	Determine a theme of a story, drama, or poem from details in the text, including how characters in a story or drama respond to challenges or how the speaker in a poem reflects upon a topic; summarize the text.
GRADE 6	GRADE 7	GRADE 8
Determine a theme or central idea of a text and how it is conveyed through particular details; provide a summary of the text distinct from personal opinions or judgments.	Determine a theme or central idea of a text and analyze its development over the course of the text, provide an objective summary of the text.	Determine a theme or central idea of a text and analyze its development over the course of the text, including its relationship to the characters, setting, and plot; provide an objective summary of the text.

Grade-level standards can be tracked according to their specific proficiency expectations based on this Bloom's/Webb's matrix.

Determine central ideas or themes of a text and analyze their development; summarize the key supporting details and ideas.

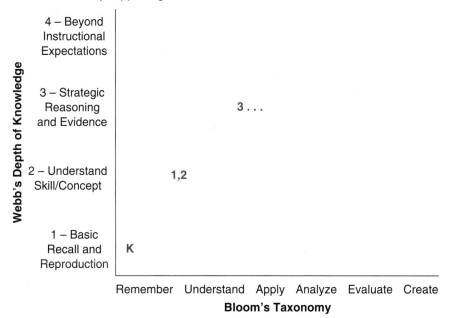

The *task complexity* for this anchor standard at each grade level increases slowly. It begins with verbs such as *Retell* and *Recount* in Grades K–2, introducing in Grades 3–5 verbs such as *Determine* and *Summarize*, and introducing *Analyze* in Grades 6–8.

The *cognitive complexity* for this anchor standard at each grade level increases moderately, allowing for prompting and support in kindergarten, and requiring they retell the story and only the central message in Grades 1–2 (DOK1–2). It is in Grade 3 that this cognitive complexity increases by requiring key details that strategically support the central message of the story. It is not until Grade 4 and up that students must write a formal summary of the central idea with evidence. From Grade 5 and up, specific details and literary perspectives are added to the context of the task complexity. It is this steady increase in cognitive complexity, not task complexity, that increases the rigor of the standards across grade levels, and it is this insight that must define and align the expectation for proficiency of this standard across grade levels.

ADAPTING ASSESSMENTS

Assessments are meant to gauge how much a student has learned, but I also see assessments as opportunities to gauge what a student is capable of mastering next. Like a reflection in a window, I see every test question as a way of gauging not only that a student has learned a standard at an expected level of proficiency but can also see the next step of that skill's development.

Formative Versus Summative

In a standards-based classroom, recognizing the differences between formative and summative assessments is critical.

FORMATIVE	SUMMATIVE
• Leveled/Tiered	• Proficient Level
• Independent or Pair/Group Task	• Independent Assessment
• As Evidence is Being Collected	• After Evidence is Collected

Defining Formative

Formative Assessments occur throughout the instructional process. As a student improves in a particular skill, it is the formative assessments that gauge that improvement over time. Later in this book, I will take this idea further by incorporating the idea that formative assessments provide profound and lasting influence on a student's personal development that has a positive effect on academic success. For now, I would like to look at the three main questions I ask myself when creating and adapting both formative and summative assessments:

- What is the standard?
- What level of proficiency is expected from the standard?
- What information from the assessment can be communicated to help the student?

For example, a fifth-grade student might be expected to master the following standard:

> **CCSS.Math.Content.5.NBT.A.2:** *Explain patterns in the number of zeros of the product when multiplying a number by powers of 10, and explain patterns in the placement of the decimal point when a decimal is multiplied or divided by a power of 10. Use whole-number exponents to denote powers of 10.*

A teacher may assign for this standard a *Level 1 Proficiency* task (or assessment) where the student is asked to identify or label the terms *base, power, exponent*, or solve a math problem involving patterns of zeroes related to multiplying a number by powers of 10, such as:

$$3.5 \times 10^4 = ?$$

If teachers have collaborated to determine that the *task complexity* of *explain* is a *Level 2 Proficiency* (though no evidence or strategic reasoning is required), then a task or assessment may require students to provide a statement (orally or in writing) describing the pattern involved in solving such a math problem.

It would then be up to the teacher to *communicate* to students the specific level of proficiency required and what this skill prepares them to do in the future. In this case, a student may consider themselves prepared to easily communicate extremely large quantities without writing an inordinate number of zeroes (e.g., stars in the sky, grains of sand, distance of the sun to each planet in miles). It is from there that the students will have the information they need to focus their efforts on the tasks specific to the standard and proficiency level.

You may want to ask yourself how many times a student must correctly respond to a Level 1 Proficiency task (such as the example above) in order to prove they are proficient at this level. How many different ways must a student be able to solve this type of math problem before a teacher considers them proficient at that particular standard or skill? This question will come up again in the following section on reporting with regard to percentages. For now, consider the design and purpose of formative and summative assessments with this question in mind.

CRITICAL POINT: Do not ignore the *task complexity* of a standard! If a student is expected to respond with understanding of a concept skill (Level 2 Proficiency), providing formative evidence that requires basic recall of information will not adequately prepare the student.

Defining Summative

Summative assessments are the proficient-based goal lines of skills or standards. These should only be provided after a student has shown success in formative tasks at developing levels of proficiency.

Summative assessments require students to independently apply their understanding of a standard in a formal assessment setting. Personally, I do rely on more traditional means of summative assessments that require students to either write or speak a response in ways that align with state testing requirements—this will not be the case for all teachers. It is important for schools to be in agreement on how proficiency will be defined for summative assessments.

Creating summative assessments for a standard initially takes some consideration and thought but can be reused and readjusted over time with ease. It is best to begin with the standard itself and define the task and context complexity of the standard. This will ensure that your assessment is set at the proficiency level required by the standard. This also removes any subjectivity to the task—make the task clear and transparent so that the student response can be communicated with confidence.

For example, consider this fourth-grade standard:

> **CCSS.ELA-Literacy.RL.4.2** *Determine a theme of a story, drama, or poem from details in the text; summarize the text.*

The *task complexity* is to not only *determine* a theme but to *summarize* the theme. The *cognitive complexity* involves not just a statement of theme but also relevant details in the text. This may be interpreted as a Level 3 Proficiency standard which tells me that, in fourth grade, one strong paragraph may be enough to show mastery of this standard. My summative assessments, therefore, may be as simple as providing a short story and a prompt. As long as the students have had opportunities to discuss themes of stories from details in the text, this summative assessment is not unreasonable. For students who have only provided more creative formative tasks such as wall art or song lyrics that describe the theme of a story (with supporting details), this summative assessment might be a stretch for them. Be careful to assess only student insight on theme and not specific formatting conventions (margins, spelling, punctuation, etc.)—as long as it is legible, you can assess their ability to analyze theme.

Assessing Proficiency

The previous fourth-grade standard for summarizing theme (RL.4.2), interpreted as a Level 3 Proficiency skill, means a student response showing a Level 3 Proficiency would consider this standard *mastered*. Depending on the grading scale used, it may be claimed the student has met 100 percent of that standard's expectations.

Students taking this same assessment that perhaps provide only a detail or two about the story and have mistaken the theme will have shown a Level 1 Proficiency, or basic recall of the story. They will not have shown an understanding of its theme (Level 2 Proficiency) enough to create an organized presentation of relevant evidence that support insight into that story's theme which would be considered a Level 3 Proficiency.

Occasionally, some students may desire to go beyond the Level 3 Proficiency expectations for a Level 3 Proficiency standard, knowing full well that Level 3

Proficiency earns them the full 100 percent credit for that standard. These students still wish to earn *extra points* and get a higher academic score.

Assigning Level 4 Proficiency

For this fourth-grade standard, a teacher may consider an additional paragraph that connects a student's theme response to another story that shares that theme or other literary elements. However, please note that this would serve only to address a different fourth-grade standard:

> **CCSS.ELA-LITERACY.RL.4.9** *Compare and contrast the treatment of similar themes and topics (e.g., opposition of good and evil) and patterns of events (e.g., the quest) in stories, myths, and traditional literature from different cultures.*

A teacher may also consider a deeper analysis of the fourth-grade theme. For example, a student might include relevant evidence that is actually the fifth-grade expectation:

> **CCSS.ELA-LITERACY.RL.5.2** *Determine a theme of a story, drama, or poem from details in the text, including how characters in a story or drama respond to challenges or how the speaker in a poem reflects upon a topic; summarize the text.*

It would be reasonable to reward a fourth-grade student response with a Level 4 Proficiency rating for this particular standard (RL.4.2) if their response to this standard's summative assessment is also addressing RL.4.9 or RL.5.2. Keep in mind that the other standard(s) being addressed would also need to receive a score that represents the appropriate level of proficiency (but not a Level 4 Proficiency) because the task assigned only specifically addressed RL.4.2.

It is also important to note the potential for marking multiple standards such as RL.4.2 (main idea) and RL.4.1 (text evidence). When the *task complexity* of a standard requires a Level 3 Proficiency response, such as the case for RL.4.2 and its expectation for evidence and reasoning of a theme, it is reasonable to mark both standards according to the proficiency shown in the student's response.

Assessment Retakes

It is common practice in a standards-based classroom for students to be allowed to retake assessments. Part of this SBG practice often includes limitations or provisions for student assessment retakes in order to motivate students not to skip formative tasks and simply retake summative assessments until they pass. The idea behind allowing students to retake an assessment is often analogized with a common real-life student experience: failing a driver's test. When a person fails their driving test, they will reflect on what was missed, and go back to take that test again (perhaps after a mandatory waiting period).

Two popular questions from teachers challenging student retakes may be: (1) what happens when students know they don't have to pass an assessment because they can take it again without consequence? and (2) will students put everything off until the last minute and submit all of their assessment submissions at the end of a reporting period as a means of abusing a retake policy? I find students approach assessments with more confidence when retakes are available without academic consequence because humans have an inherent desire to succeed even if they do not show it in behaviors that we may recognize. It is a positive sign that a student cares enough about their education to try an assessment again—it is illogical and emotionally draining to choose to retake an assessment knowing failure is guaranteed.

However, when the expectation is to submit reasonable evidence of reflection (formative task) before requesting a summative assessment retake, it becomes less about expecting the academic proficiency of the student prior to a retake and more about coaching a student's habits and increasing that student's confidence in passing a summative assessment retake. It is important that this shift toward retakes in an SBG classroom be recognized because there will always be a potential for overwhelming teacher expectations if reasonable student expectations for retakes are not simple, transparent, and consistent. For this reason alone, shifting toward test retakes in this way requires as much shift from the teacher's perspective as it does the students, parents, and a school's administration.

REPORTING PROFICIENCY

For this section, the most important difference between reporting formative and summative assessments must be reiterated. *Summative assessments* communicate progress of student mastery of each standard or skill at a particular level of proficiency and are meant to provide feedback to parents and administration. *Formative assessments* represent the process of student learning of each standard or skill and are meant to provide feedback to students for their own accountability and growth.

Standards-Based Proficiency Within a Traditional Percentage-Based Reporting System

Disclaimer: It is my personal opinion that percentage-based and letter-based reporting systems are less effective in communicating student learning and that these processes are intended to make it easier to give fast feedback for increased quantities of students in classrooms. It is not my intention for the following section to promote the use of percentage-based reporting systems in schools.

A standards-based approach can exist within a traditional system of reporting a final percentage or letter grade score. A well-structured standards-based approach can help students trace back a final percentage or letter grade to a standards-based breakdown of skills. This means that, hypothetically, a student who receives a score of 71 percent (or a C- respectively) on their report card can approach their teacher and know which skills make up that percentage of skill mastery. More important, this simultaneously highlights the breakdown of the 29 percent of skills and standards they did not master. This makes it much more transparent for the student and their parents what exactly the student can do to improve their final score—extra work on standards they have already mastered will not improve their final score. This increases the accountability on the part of the student for ensuring they master the skills necessary for the next grade level.

One key aspect in this reverse engineering of percentage to standards is the decision (as a teacher, group, or school) over which standards are most critical in preparing for subsequent grade levels. This decision may spark discussion about whether standards can and should be grouped into a single skill for reporting, and which standards may align with other domains within a subject or across subject content areas.

Another key aspect involves an awareness of past student perspectives attempting to manipulate the grade reporting system. A student may be comfortable asking that a B be raised to an A by requesting *extra credit* or inquire about resubmitting various formative-style tasks (e.g., worksheets, practice problems) in order to raise a final score for that reporting period. If the reported grade is only based on summative assessments, and student access to summative assessment is based on their completion of formative tasks as evidence of readiness, then the focus shifts from what students must *do* (worksheets, practice problems, participation) to what students must *learn* (mastery of a skill or concept at a level of proficiency clearly defined). This shift is a part of this key aspect teachers will want to reflect upon and discuss over time.

Provisions for Using Percentages

Percentage as a grading tool for formative tasks is covered in a previous section of this chapter. It is important to remember that percentages can easily become misleading when proficiency of a standard needs to be communicated. The following table refers to a scenario in which a summative assessment has five specific questions, parts, sections, or divided tasks that target a single standard that meets Level 2 Proficiency:

GRADING AN ASSESSMENT TO DEPTH OF PROFICIENCY				
4	Beyond Instructional Expectations	5 correct = 100% correct 4 correct = 80% correct	"Proficient" or "Met Expectation"	*Mark student proficient and assess again at higher level of proficiency if necessary or move on to the next skill or standard.*
3	Strategic Reasoning and Evidence	3 correct = 60% correct	"Near Proficient" or "Nearly Met Expectation"	*Follow up with student to gauge clarity of question and response to determine proficiency of the specific skill of standard.*
2	Understanding Skill/Concept			
1	Basic Recall or Reproduction	2 correct = 40% correct 1 correct = 20% correct	"Not Proficient" or "Can Meet Expectation"	*Do not mark student proficient and allow for subsequent version of assessment to be taken pending evidence of practice.*

Using this table as an example, a student with four or five correct responses may be considered *Proficient* in that particular standard. A student who shows three correct responses may be considered *Near Proficient* and may only need to review what was missed in order to determine if more evidence of practice is needed. A student who provides only one or two correct responses may not have adequately worked through the concept or skill and perhaps has an underlying misunderstanding and requires intervention before attempting that assessment again.

Percentage Precautions

There are two common dangers when using percentages for summative assessments:

1. The hard line for defining *passing* and *failing* with percentages is not always the same for every teacher and school and between various standards and skills.

2. Percentages communicate little information regarding what was and was not learned.

Percentages can be a complicated tool for communicating student progress. Students able to correctly respond to four out of five tasks on a summative assessment may have a strong understanding but, depending on how the assessment was designed, may be missing a critical aspect of a skill. Communicating a *passing* score of 80 percent provides little to no incentive for a student to reflect.

The following table illustrates an important question: How many correctly answered questions does it take for a student to prove proficient? For a school that sets a percentage hard line for *passing* at 70 percent, answering all but two or three results in a failing or near-failing grade. It is critical that assessments be created with intention, so that if each *point* is representing a different skill, task, or process, then a student score may communicate progress in each. However, if all of the questions on an assessment focus on the same particular skill or process, a student who correctly responds four out of five times in a row (80 percent) versus four out of six times in a row (66 percent) should not be the difference between *passing* and *failing* without an opportunity to reflect on potential student misunderstanding.

PERCENTAGE BREAKDOWN DILEMMA

Question: How many correctly answered questions does it take for a student to prove *proficient*?

Answer: It depends on the quality of the assessment questions and student responses, not the number of questions a student happens to answer correctly.

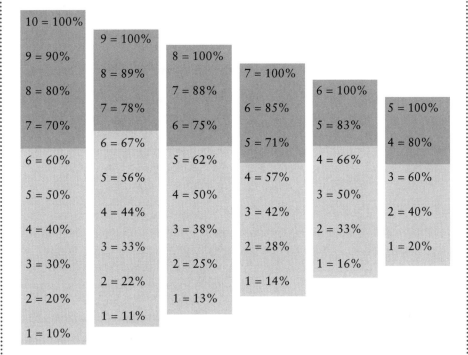

Proficiency is not a percentage point.

A transparent and well-organized standards-based approach can support a percentage score by providing a means for communicating what percentage of skills or standards have and have not been mastered.

CURRICULA AND RESOURCES

A school will often ask for teacher feedback on purchasing a school-wide curriculum from publishing companies. There is often some amount of miscommunication between teachers when selecting curricula and supplemental resources depending on the mastery of standards, proficiency levels, and assessment and reporting practices across the classrooms. It is important that a school's staff has gone through these aspects of a standards-based approach and has come to a consensus on these issues. When presented with a choice of curricula, such a consensus will provide the intent and purpose for discussing the value of a curricula.

When a curriculum is chosen, teachers with a standards-based mindset may flip through the literature collections, math practice workbooks, science project activities, history textbooks, and pick out the resources and materials that support the levels of proficiency for the standards in their grade level. The biggest obstacle is teachers having the time to go through all the curricula material to know where everything is so that they can address specific student needs as they arise at any point in the school year.

The following three questions may help focus the selection and use of a purchased curriculum.

1. What do students need to master this year's standards?

The resources I provide to my students begin and end with the standards I am assigned to teach. For example, if I am assigned a grade level that introduces a specific skill for the first time, I will want to have a class set of manipulatives that address that skill. For a comprehensive curriculum, it is important to take the time to find and organize resources by standard or skill so that, throughout the year, resources can be found as needed.

When considering standards such as the seventh-grade literature standard (RL.7.5) which asks students to analyze how a drama or poem's form or structure contributes to its meaning, the resources can be wide ranging. Are there particular texts in the curriculum that would benefit from comparison of meaning across genres and styles? Is there a particular graphic organizer included to help students to compare and contrast? Are there theatrical considerations included in the curriculum? Depending on the teacher's approach to analyzing literature, the question of what student resources are needed for mastery will require time to dig and discuss. How deep a teacher wants to go into a particular standard will also entail a level of materials and resources that will need to be found, organized, and provided to students with intent of learning that specific standard at expected levels of proficiency.

2. What does my classroom need for my students to master the standards?

This question considers how much accountability for student learning will be shared between the teacher and the students. This will help determine how much of my classroom will be devoted to either reference-style decoration or more interactive data-driven wall design. Personally, I am always looking to further my classroom's interactivity between students and their progress toward standards mastery. (I go into greater detail about that in a later chapter, *Self-Directed Learning*). For this section, however, it is important to define the purpose of my classroom as it relates to the relationship I want to build between students, their progress, and my style of instruction and support.

Focusing areas of the room on promoting the shift from teacher to student ownership of learning could involve room designs that include data walls, writing walls, idea walls, or reflection walls.

Interactive student data walls promote empathy, accountability, and a collective ownership of learning. This kind of data wall lists all objective academic goals and allows students to track their progress together as a class. This not only allows daily reminders of their individual goals and progress, but communicates to each other who has mastered a particular skill and may be able to provide assistance.

Writing walls promote long-term task completion as a single task such as an ELA essay or science project plan. This allows students to share with each other what is being studied in class while also making it possible to quickly address any issues students may be having with their tasks quickly and efficiently (by the teacher and by students).

Idea and reflection walls promote academic discussion as students develop and post new ideas, thoughts, questions, and concerns, for other students to also consider. These walls are difficult for students who are either not used to opening themselves up or feel there's little academic value with regard to their final grade. However, these walls can provide sparks of interest for students who may have forgotten that talking about interesting things about this world is a big reason for going to school. These walls also allow teachers to help shape those ideas into samples and evidence that may also be submitted for evidence of a standard.

A common concern from parents (and some colleagues) is confidentiality of student data and the effect on student anxiety that displaying student data on classroom walls can have. However, in the years that I have personally used data wall charts in my classroom, I have found the opposite occurs. Transparency of student learning puts my students in a position to question and share their progress with each other that supports empathy versus sympathy and has helped build friendships of respect and equity.

3. **How accessible to students are resources in the classroom?**

This question focuses on the level of control a teacher chooses to maintain over the classroom and its resources. Keeping all resources in a teacher-only cabinet that is used only with their permission creates a different type of classroom than one that provides labeled resources for students to freely access as needed. This question over accessibility of resources is important because it directly affects the style of classroom management.

A high amount of direct instruction that follows a traditional model of engagement, instruction, guided modeling, independent practice, and an exit ticket (for example) might require a classroom setting with table groups and table resources that the teacher distributes and maintains with intention each day. In this example, the teacher is the sole proprietor of resources and the students will look to the teacher for all questions and concerns regarding materials. A low amount of direct instruction may result in a much higher percentage of peer-based learning activities as the means for instruction and practice. This environment might require all resources for all standards to be readily available by all students throughout the year. My students then have the majority of control over the resources in the room. The goal for the teacher in such an environment is to focus their efforts on teaching accountability of shared materials for the benefit of all students rather than benefiting individual students.

A hybrid of these two examples may be adjusted to the age and developmental stages of the students. Over time (weeks or months, depending on the class), students can be taught to recognize the value of resources as each target specific standards that students must master. By bringing into the classroom only those resources that target standards-based learning of my grade level, I will have prepared a strong base for providing students adequate opportunities to master the grade-level standards.

CHAPTER 2

Social-Emotional Learning

All students experience eight components of social-emotional development in an ebb and flow of developing stages. As students experience a difficult academic topic, they will often be working through concepts of self, such as self-efficacy, goal-setting, and coping strategies. As students experience challenges working within and between different social groups, they will likely work through concepts of empathy, perspective, and conflict resolution. It is also common for students to experience external challenges outside of their control involving school- and community-wide responsibilities and consequences, the value of reward as a result of their own responsibility, and the effects their actions have on their community. Students master these skills primarily through experience so it is critical that the classroom teacher be well versed in these areas as students find themselves in various challenging situations.

It is important to remember that social and emotional learning must not be *graded* in the traditional sense with an objective hard line of mastery but as a fluid development of awareness and ongoing progress. There is an inherent inequity among student experience and such ongoing development of each component that expecting teachers to objectively define and identify in students a *proficiency* is unreasonable for both the teacher and the students.

As teachers, our role is to monitor and adjust our approach toward supporting individual students based on observations of student development through the various SEL components. For example, students who are quiet or shy may not show a public proficiency of certain social and interpersonal skills. On the other hand, the outgoing and talkative students may not illustrate certain coping strategies for more intimate settings between peers. This doesn't mean that any of these students are not proficient in those areas—it may be that these aspects of their development are simply not being perceived by us as teachers, as observers.

Whatever grade level I am assigned to teach, being able to recognize each component of social and emotional learning begins with my awareness that each component exists in all of my students. In the following sections, I look at each component and consider the value of each as it relates to the classroom. As the value of each component is recognized, I can think forward to how each of my students may be developing through stages of each component. Then, as I prepare my lessons throughout the year, I can adjust the learning environment to meet the needs of my students as they develop through these components at their pace.

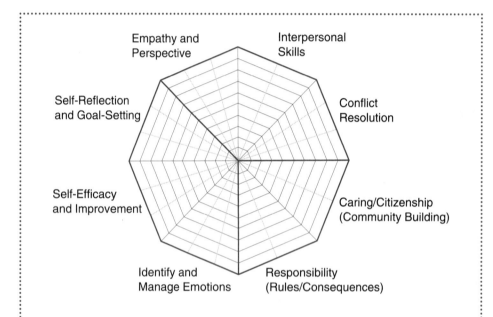

EIGHT SEL COMPONENTS

SELF-AWARENESS AND MANAGEMENT

- Identify and Manage Emotions
- Self-Efficacy and Improvement
- Self-Reflection and Goal-Setting

SOCIAL AWARENESS AND RELATIONSHIPS

- Empathy and Perspective
- Interpersonal Skills
- Conflict Resolution

SOCIETAL AWARENESS

- Responsibility (Rules and Consequences)
- Caring/Citizenship (Community Building)

SELF-AWARENESS AND MANAGEMENT

The Collaborative for Academic, Social, and Emotional Learning (CASEL) connects self-awareness with *growth mindset* as students learn their strengths and limitations with a well-grounded sense of confidence and optimism. CASEL separately describes self-management as the ability to effectively manage stress, control impulses, and motivate oneself to set and achieve goals. This book's approach toward self-awareness and management combines and reorganizes these CASEL competencies into three components: Identifying and Managing Emotions, Self-Efficacy and Improvement, and Self-Reflection and Goal-Setting.

Identifying and Managing Emotions

This first component is a great place to begin when preparing for a school year. Depending on the age or grade level, I may be looking for basic, compound, or complex emotions being expressed in either simple or complex situations that can be managed with various coping strategies. These differences depend on what grade level has been assigned to the teacher and what experiences and social-emotional support students have received in prior years.

This is a good place to mention a rare but still important critique I have received from teachers regarding social and emotional learning. I have heard teachers ask how it is that, as an English or math teacher, they are also expected to meet the role of a *child psychologist*. The jump from social and emotional learning in a classroom to the role of child psychologist is quite great. My response typically involves the comparison of content mastery as an English or math teacher to that of their content mastery of being a socially and emotionally well-balanced adult. I also like to include how we, as teachers, do not teach academics—we teach humans about academics. We have been given a responsibility for teaching a room full of children who may not have mastered certain social and emotional skills and that it is in the best interest of all teachers and all students to provide social and emotional support for the sake of school-wide student success.

> *We don't teach academics—we teach humans.*

For our youngest students, I may be looking for recognition of basic emotions, sharing various feelings that are attributed to these basic emotions, and identifying simple coping strategies such as patience and self-talk in simple scenarios. Often, these strategies have not been taught to students before they enter kindergarten and may be prone to fits of shame and doubt that can hinder their academic success if not identified and supported.

As students get older, I may again be looking for recognition of basic emotions but through more complex interconnected feelings that involve personal trials and tribulations that are mixed with years of past development. For these older students, it is important to recognize that while complex feelings may be shown through basic emotional physical responses, they may not be ready to discuss such complex feelings and, instead, may need to be confident in their understanding of those basic feelings and emotions before they will be able or willing to discuss them. For this reason, it is important to provide the language and context for emotions, feelings, and coping strategies.

Basic Emotions

There are two theorists that I personally highlight when discussing emotions. The first is Robert Plutchik and his psychoevolutionary theory of basic emotions which states there are eight basic emotions: fear, anger, sadness, joy, disgust, surprise, trust, and anticipation. The second is Paul Ekman and he includes only six basic emotions: anger, happiness, surprise, disgust, sadness, and fear. Ekman's work has since been used to create an Atlas of Emotions, imagined by the Dalai Lama, that focuses on five basic emotions: *Joy, Anger, Fear, Sadness,* and *Disgust.* In my experience, these five words cover the majority of feelings and situations that arise in classrooms, so I devote my energy to utilizing this arrangement as my primary source.

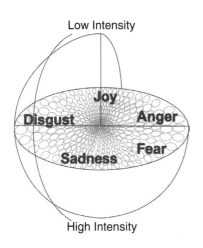

Disgust

Low Intensity

Aversion
strategy: evaluate harmfulness,
let aversion dissolve

Dislike/Distaste
strategy: evaluate ethical issue,
generate compassion

Repugnance
strategy: evaluate harmfulness,
let aversion dissolve

Loathing (self)
strategy: healthy regret spurs
improvement, healing

Loathing (others)
strategy: adopt healthful outlook

Loathing (others)
strategy: calmly avoid situation
adopt caring outlook

High Intensity

Joy

Low Intensity

Schadenfreude
("harm-joy")
strategy: recognize destructive
effects, benevolence

Pride
strategy: humility, perspective,
interdependency

[Impediments]
unnecessarily warring,
see in the negative, pessimism,
envy, arrogance, vanity
narcissism, jealousy, regret

Ecstacy
strategy: be aware of harm
related to this state

High Intensity

Fear

Low Intensity

Trepidation
strategy: calming self-talk

Nervousness
strategy: focus on cause
effect, solution

Anxiety
strategy: focus on present,
let go of past/future

Dread
strategy: focus on what can
possibly be done

Panic
strategy: seek mitigating factors
of possible causes

Horror/Terror
strategy: focus on solution both
immediate and after

High Intensity

Anger

Low Intensity

Annoyance
strategy: empathy

Frustration
strategy: empathy, "letting go"

Argumentativeness
strategy: empathy, benevolence

Exasperation
strategy: understanding larger
causes and conditions

Vengefulness
strategy: contemplate negative
effects of reverge

Fury
strategy: take a step back
self-awareness

High Intensity

Sadness

Low Intensity

Disappointment
strategy: sadness is natural
find peace within

Distraught
strategy: pay homage to loss
w/ positive productivity

Helplessness
strategy: pay homage to loss
w/ positive productivity

Misery
strategy: pay homage to loss
w/ positive productivity

Despair
strategy: pay homage to loss
w/ positive productivity

Anguish
strategy: realize things and people
are impermanent by nature

High Intensity

In my personal experience, the most difficult situations for me as a teacher have involved emotions that I understand the least. I recognize in myself, as a human, an instinctual *negative* association toward emotions other than joy. When a student expresses a basic emotion other than joy, my initial reaction is to *remedy* that emotion. However, any misinterpretations I have toward the value of (what I associate as) negative emotions have made some situations more difficult to deal with than others. Therefore, *understanding basic emotions is not only a student expectation, but a human expectation* that requires common language and healthy communication between all involved in any experience.

Identification of emotions and feelings is one social-emotional aspect of the whole-child approach. The most important takeaway from this one aspect is the idea that emotions are physical representations and are measurable on a scale of intensity. Feelings are associated with at least one emotion and the language we use to discuss feelings must be clarified in order to determine coping strategies for the various situations.

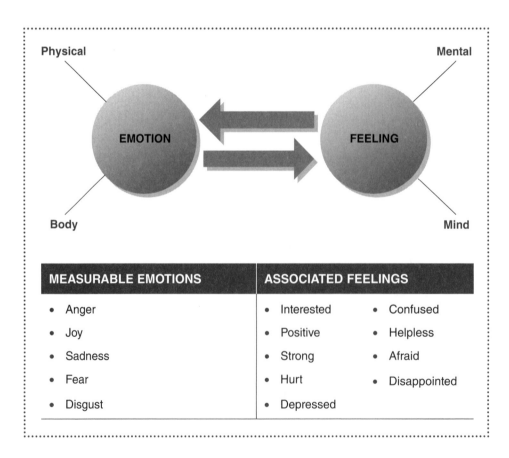

MEASURABLE EMOTIONS	ASSOCIATED FEELINGS	
• Anger	• Interested	• Confused
• Joy	• Positive	• Helpless
• Sadness	• Strong	• Afraid
• Fear	• Hurt	• Disappointed
• Disgust	• Depressed	

Because an emotion is the first thing we see expressed by a student, our understanding of that emotion will serve to guide an initial response. For younger students, we may only expect them to use a basic language for identifying and communicating basic emotions. For students at the early elementary grade levels, guiding the use of language such as *angry*, *sad*, or *happy* develops a common language that expresses how they feel in a group setting. As students get older, the range of emotions will begin to expand as their experiences and language become more complex. For each basic emotion, students will begin to experience ranges of intensity for this emotion that is important to identify so that we can adjust our approach toward classroom management in such a way that incorporates changing needs.

Feelings

The name we give an emotion only serves to label what is ultimately a physical manifestation of feelings. As a student shows an emotion such as anger or a compound emotion, such as sadness and anger, the student may describe the emotion as *feeling angry*. However, as I work with a student in deciphering the source of the anger, it may be that the student isn't only angry, but, more specifically feels frustrated, confused, or sullen about an event that happened in their life and unsure how to express those feelings.

Each year, I develop a shared language with my students to describe feelings. It requires that I have an inventory of words that can be used for various situations. Depending on the grade level I am assigned to teach, I may adjust these words to account for simple or complex situations. I may also consider that early elementary students may only need simple words for simple feelings even though they are showing intense emotions; middle and high school students may need a wider range of words that account for multiple needs as their circumstances become more complex.

There are many lists of words for various feelings available on the internet. However, the words I choose to use with my students are decided upon before I begin my school year and are consistent throughout the year. This allows students and teachers that enter my classroom from other classrooms or other schools to share this language and participate in using this language as situations arise.

ANGER	JOY	SADNESS	FEAR	DISGUST
Touchy	Mellow	Unhappy	Timid	Dislike/Distaste
Annoyed	Pleasant	Disappointed	Unsure	Adverse
Perturbed	Glad	Blue	Nervous	Repulsed
Upset	Satisfied	Melancholy	Apprehensive	Revolted
Mad	Gratified	Somber	Frightened	Revulsed
Frustrated	Cheerful	Distressed	Threatened	Repugnant
Irate	Overjoyed	Sorrowful	Frantic	Despise
Seething	Thrilled	Miserable	Petrified	Hate
Outraged	Excited	Agonized	Horrified	Loathe
Furious	Elated	Depressed	Terrified	Abhor

Any list of feelings is going to be inherently subjective as words may take on different meanings in different contexts. Be aware that a student may say they are simply *annoyed* at another student while they are showing an extreme level of emotional intensity. These moments when students express intense emotion may not seem like the best time to have a lesson on *shades of meaning*, but it is the time to include in the discussion with that student a recognition of emotional intensity so that an appropriate coping mechanism may be discussed.

We may see people physically emote based on how they learn to associate feelings. Two people feeling disappointed may emote either sadness or anger. The point is the importance in recognizing how a person's emotional reactions may not resemble how they're feeling.

Coping Strategies

There are many different approaches, strategies, and products to teach people how to cope with different emotions. For me as a classroom teacher, I often try to find approaches that develop *empathetic reasoning* or those that build upon *altruistic habits*. When a student exhibits an overwhelming emotional response to an event, the strategy for coping with that emotion will not only address a desire to help themselves gain control of that overwhelming emotion but also recognize the benefits such control has on their learning environment (*empathetic reasoning*). At the same time, student peers must also be taught the value in recognizing and supporting a student who is actively coping with overwhelming emotion in a shared learning environment for no purpose other than to support that student (*altruistic habits*). When the goal of a classroom is to ensure a safe and positive learning environment, strategies must be made available to all students for coping and assisting with the control of their own emotions.

The goal of coping strategies is not to resolve conflicts or solve problems. Strategies allow people to maintain control over their physical reactions so they may be able to address the causes of those emotions as reasonably, safely, and respectfully as possible. The following strategies are not the only strategies, nor are they to be considered the best, but are a few that I have had experience in teaching my own students in upper elementary and middle school.

COPING STRATEGIES	
Deep Breathing	All emotions benefit from focusing on breathing to help calm the body. A timed breathing pattern can help a person cognitively control their physical reaction to overwhelming emotion.
	Breathe in for five seconds, hold for one second, breathe out for seven seconds. Repeat.

COPING STRATEGIES	
Positive Self-Talk	For sadness or disgust, focusing on positive self-efficacy can keep a person from spiraling through negative physical reactions.
	I am good at sports and people cheer for me. I help others with their homework and they're thankful. I bought a friend's book of poems to support them and they felt good about that.
Sensory Countdown	For anger or fear, focusing on immediate surroundings can help refocus attention and interrupt unhealthy patterns of thought.
	Stay still and notice (5) five things you can see, (4) four things you can touch/feel, (3) three things you can hear, (2) two things you can smell, and (1) one thing you can taste.
Benevolence	For anger or sadness, focusing on altruistic or benevolent behaviors that benefit others can help relieve tension and maintain open roads for communication.
	Recognize and communicate the value in a person or find a way to ease a person's stress.

Self-Efficacy and Improvement

This second component of Self-Awareness and Management is mostly about value—the value of self and the value of people, places, actions, and reactions.

As a classroom teacher, beginning with younger children, identifying value is important. It is common to teach students to recognize helpful people such as police, firefighters, teachers, and doctors. In upper elementary grade levels, similar value may be extended to those in their lives that not only help them academically and otherwise but perhaps more importantly, they are able to communicate ways they reciprocate help in return. At the middle and high school grade levels, an example of values may begin to address more abstract and complex ideas such as the value of community outreach programs assisting families in need by obtaining necessary resources for healthy living. Nonetheless, identifying value at various stages in a student's development is an important aspect of social-emotional learning that develops through the grade levels as students get older and their worldviews become more complex.

Self-Efficacy and Behavior

This idea of self-efficacy and value connects to student behaviors. There are two important factors when addressing self-efficacy as it relates to behaviors:

1. Every human wants to be liked.
2. Every human wants to be successful.

If one of these two factors are not being satisfied, the other may be used to overcompensate within a student's self-efficacy—their sense of value of themselves and those around them. While these two statements may seem highly subjective since the degree of being *liked* or being *successful* is different for every individual, it is exactly because of this subjectivity that these two statements can be seen across classrooms over time.

From these two statements, I can determine that if a student is not proving successful in a given task, they may resolve to amusing their peers, occasionally at a time or place most inappropriate and thus receive the most praise from their peers. Likewise, if a student seems to be ill-favored by any number of other students, they may go out of their way to prove their superiority over those students, occasionally at a time or place most inappropriate but will receive the most attention.

More often than not, minor classroom management issues can often be addressed by identifying one of these two aspects of self-efficacy. Keep in mind that the challenge is not only identifying student behaviors by these two statements but recognizing that the immediacy of a logical and predetermined punishment for a negative student behavior may do little to address a student's developing self-efficacy—their sense of value in both themselves and those around them. The idea of addressing negative student behavior through self-efficacy might begin with a school's flowchart of consequences but we as teachers may need to go deeper into patterns of behaviors that reflect how these two statements may need to be addressed in classrooms.

Developing and Interpreting Values

Identifying the value of human resources and services is only one aspect of this development. Interpreting the value of ideas, actions, and expectations can quickly become more complex. For example, a school-wide framework of values might begin with expecting students to be *safe* and *respectful*. These two words can be subjectively, and at times inconsistently, interpreted as values. For example, the idea of being safe for one person may be considered unsafe by another. Now substitute the words safe and unsafe with respect and disrespect and the same will apply. This can go even further when you consider the values reflected in a person's reaction to what others may or may not perceive as safe or respectful.

The goal is not to develop a detailed code or encyclopedia of values, behaviors, and interpretations. Rather, it is more about focusing on what a value means to each person, determine a shared language through experience over time, and discuss how it can be applied in the context of various situations. Even when a situation involves two students whose actions both contradict the values of the school, yet pointing a guilty finger at the other, an agreed upon shared interpretation of a school's framework of values can insist that the students recognize their own momentary forgetfulness of one value or another and discuss as a group whether their own actions and reactions played a role in the conflict. When a school's framework for social and emotional learning is internalized by teachers as part of a school's vision, conflict may not immediately devolve to punitive measures without reason.

Teachers benefit from reflecting on the values being instilled when student misbehavior is addressed in our own classrooms. For me, personally, safety and respect are important values, but so are kindness and responsibility which serve subtly different purposes in different situations. It requires much deliberation on our part as teachers to distinguish which value (or how much of each different value) may be put in to question with any given situation. It becomes less about the encyclopedic number of possible situations and more about my own clarity for each value and its purpose.

Values such as *fairness*, *kindness*, *responsibility*, and *respect* can have ranging interpretations. Whatever values a school or classroom chooses to instill will need to be defined with shared language and be provided ongoing opportunities to share unique student situations where these values may have been difficult to address. The shared language does not mean strict definitions for values—this would hinder the ability to adjust to unique situations that arise. It is important that a school's staff and classroom teachers are able to communicate these values quickly and succinctly in their own words to ensure situations are dealt with consistently across a school campus.

Student and staff accountability of values is a very difficult conversation. School staff are the arbiters of a school's values and social expectations. To hold students to higher expectations than adults are being held can result in a climate of distrust. Students may develop conflicting perspectives toward those values being reiterated if those values are not being modeled. An open culture of communication among staff can result from healthy development of the same social and emotional skills discussed in this chapter.

Self-Reflection and Goal-Setting

This third component of Self-Awareness and Management is the most visible component. This is a critical area that requires consistency of instruction and practice on the part of both the student and the teacher. A highly transparent example of this is seen in students of music, art, dance, theater, or athletics, all of which require physical representations of an observed product. In music, the moment a student plays a note on their instrument they can hear and are provided with immediate feedback on their physical performance of the instrument. The moment they sit down to practice, they have decided how long to practice, what exactly they expect to get out of practicing, and, once they are done practicing, how many more times they expect to practice before they are ready to perform. This consistency of self-reflection and goal-setting is what makes these extracurricular subjects so demanding yet so important for academic teachers to understand and support—not just in words but in their actions.

SMART Goals

My classroom, when it's perfect, is filled with students who have set goals that are specific, measurable, attainable, relevant, and time-based. However, it is important that people know my classroom is not perfect! While I do promote goal-setting and tracking of student progress, and many students eventually embrace one style of goal-setting or another, it is difficult for every single student to view this goal-setting process as valuable enough to commit the necessary time and energy every day. This is an important challenge of goal-setting that, to be clear, must not be seen as a misbehavior or act of oppositional defiance. Instead, classrooms can offer students opportunities to experiment with various goal-setting strategies and experience the value of self-reflection when looking back at the progress they've made over time. Even for those students who ultimately choose not to set goals for themselves for long periods of time, the cost of that choice is the accountability placed on them through ongoing discussion of progress with academic standards.

One strategy for goal-setting is the SMART Goals approach, which has a generally accepted origin from November 1981 in Spokane, Washington. George T. Doran, a consultant and former Director of Corporate Planning for Washington Water Power Company, published a paper titled "There's a S.M.A.R.T. Way to Write Management's Goals and Objectives." Teachers are encouraged to refer to this source and consider the value of the five measures that make up this goal-setting approach.

S.M.A.R.T. GOALS	
Specific	What academic standard do I want to master?
Measurable	How will I track progress of this goal over time?
Attainable	What resources will I need for me to reach this goal?
Relevant	Is this short-term goal important to my long-term goals?
Time-Oriented	Are there dates set for self-reflection of progress toward this goal?

At the start of a school year, teachers may expect very few students to be able to develop SMART goals independently. Teachers that wish to train this strategy into their students will want to include daily goals in this SMART goal format for the first few weeks (or months) of a school year. This could include having every student produce clearly designed goals for the simplest routine tasks to be completed each day until these simple goals can be written out quickly without much thought. The tediousness of this exercise will eventually become apparent when these simplest of daily tasks can be verbally clarified and recalled throughout the day without the need for referencing a written record of that goal. However, as the weeks pass and the academic expectations become more demanding, the nature of these SMART goals becomes almost frustrating to students as they work to determine the goal of more demanding tasks. It is at this point that the SMART goals become more than a tedious exercise and, over time, more students begin to recognize that the time they spend writing out these goals focuses attention on the reason they are at school—to master academic skills and assist their peers in doing the same.

SMART Goals as a strategy is only one approach to developing self-reflection and goal-setting. There are many resources that provide students opportunities to practice setting a goal and monitoring progress. The quality of the approach will depend not only on the creator of the resource but the ability of the teacher to adapt it to specific student needs. Whatever the approach, we as teachers will want to not only celebrate goal completion but also that goal's completion as it sparks another related goal that takes the student further into that skill's development (or a related skill in that grade level). For the student who does not succeed in reaching a goal must not be allowed to consider themselves done with that goal but be guided in adjusting and attempting again that goal as a means of developing perseverance. Whatever resource a teacher provides to help guide students in goal-setting, ensuring that the goal has objective qualities that can be measured for success will allow the student to determine what about their approach to meeting their goal did or did not work. While I prefer to utilize the SMART Goals approach, it is encouraged that students be allowed to adapt other approaches to goal-setting that provide healthy parameters for achieving their goals. It is important that students not be corrected on their particular style of goal-setting but instead be given opportunities to explain how their approach might be improved upon as they move forward with other goals.

"Want" Versus "Need"

When a student is deciding if they have met their goal, perhaps as determined by SMART goal metrics, the conversation of whether the goal they achieved produced something that they *want* versus what they *need* can be challenging. The difference is not so much in the quality or quantity of the goal achieved and the product produced but more a question centered on the student's value of the produced work. In other words, goal-setting may not always be about what the student *wants* if what the student wants is not also what the student *needs*. This, I believe, is the crux of a student's inner conflict toward valuing goal-setting and self-reflection.

This is the difficult aspect of the SMART goal because it does require discussion of value and self-improvement on the part of the student. This idea does not come easy for all students as it represents a pattern of inward reflection that students may not have observed in their homes or from their peers.

It may take more than half a school year for some students to accept this idea of *value* toward wants versus needs before development of goal-setting habits can begin taking hold. For many students, the value for which they see their own product will remain low enough that the quality of work they produce requires minimal effort.

As a teacher, it is important that I continue to reflect on the following idea: when students require of themselves less effort, they are procuring less chance of failure and constant revisions that can feel like a series of failures on their part. For me to demand a student raise their personal value system to meet my own value system as a teacher can have the opposite effect of that desired. It is my intention to incorporate this clarification of *want* versus *need* over a long series of student tasks, to allow the student to consider whether their work is providing opportunities to improve, without external judgment, for the sake of increasing the student's value as that student continues to improve.

It is my belief that offering all students opportunities to consider how they, as the student, can make choices to improve themselves, knowing that it will take a long time to improve, is something that will benefit them beyond the one school year they spend with me. It is important to recognize that we, as teachers, provide students opportunities to recognize and reflect on the products they produce. This allows for those students to connect the feeling of *wanting* to achieve a goal with *needing* certain skills to succeed in order to reach more rewarding goals in the future.

SOCIAL-AWARENESS AND RELATIONSHIPS

The Collaborative for Academic, Social, and Emotional Learning (CASEL) connects social-awareness with empathy and perspective and the ability to recognize diversity and respect for others. CASEL separately describes relationship skills as the ability to communicate and cooperate with others in ways that support teamwork and strong relationships. The three components of this book's approach to social-awareness and relationships combines and reorganizes these CASEL competencies into three components: Empathy and Perspective, Interpersonal Skills, and Conflict Resolution.

Empathy and Perspective

This fourth component is, in my opinion, the most difficult and most critical aspect of social and emotional learning. It also has the most relevance to academic success in that so many academic standards require a student to see a topic from a point of view other than their own. The concept of empathetic reasoning is often lost when an individual's purpose is centered on their own success, whether it be professional or personal. Developing a sense of empathy and perspective requires not only direct instruction but experience and opportunity for self-reflection over a long period of time. The earlier a student receives guidance in empathy and perspective, the more internalized the concepts will become as the student develops from kindergarten up through high school. As for us teachers, we have developed some sense of empathy but may not have had that sense actualized and communicated in a way where we feel confident to teach it. At this, I say, do not be afraid of it and learn to recognize that your own development in empathy and perspective can be shared with your students as you improve your own self and social awareness and management of skills detailed in this chapter.

Sympathy Versus Empathy

There is a common misconception between sympathy and empathy. When somebody slips, a person watching might laugh or they might passively ask "are you okay?" However, when somebody falls and gets physically injured, that same person watching might comment out-loud how much that must have hurt or inhale sharply through their teeth as they hold whichever body part they just watched being injured.

These differences in an observer's reactions demonstrates the difference between sympathy and empathy. Sympathy is the recognition that somebody else feels a certain way. Empathy is the ability to internalize how somebody else feels in that moment. It is important to note that the awareness of these differences is important as it does drive a student's ability to connect with others in more meaningful ways and can guide behaviors and reactions to situations in various contexts.

To understand how this works, consider your own wants and needs for friendship. Consider the friend that not only comments when you get hurt but shares the pain that you feel when you get hurt. That connection is important for all students to understand and exercise, even if it requires a teacher's guidance in recognizing and developing that awareness.

Empathetic Capacity

The most challenging aspect of this difference between sympathy versus empathy is the idea that, while empathy may be rechargeable, it is not a boundless resource. The capacity for empathy may not be the same in all people and developing that capacity is dependent on variables beyond a classroom teacher's control. That doesn't mean empathy should not be taught; it means awareness of empathetic capacity should be considered when dealing with a student who may be reacting poorly to another student's unfortune.

For example, when a person falls, one person may laugh while another may run over and check to see if they are hurt. The person that chooses to react through quiet laughter to themselves may not be completely wrong in their reaction as they simply may not hold much value for the person that fell. As awful as that may sound, I have come to recognize that humans often learn to reserve more of their empathy for certain individuals that they personally value.

Providing guidance for students to understand the difference between sympathy and empathy becomes quite powerful when you consider the effects those students may have as they become adults. This, hopefully, will cause questions to arise in schools and communities about how we want children to see this difference between sympathy and empathy. How deeply do we want students to access this emotional energy for the care of others? How far do we want our students to spend this emotional energy for the benefit of themselves and those around them?

If we as teachers were to place concentric rings around each student showing how far that student should be guided in spending their emotional energy, how far out from their immediate family and friends would you consider appropriate for your students to exercise empathy? Would you consider a single tight circle around each student as your students are solely focused on themselves? Would you consider two or three concentric circles around each student which include those in their immediate surrounding? Perhaps enough concentric circles reach outward to their community? Would they be circular waves that include some but not others? This then becomes a critical component in the culture of a classroom which feeds a school and its surrounding community.

"Power of Perspective"

Perspective is a different but similar idea. Perspective is the view from that of the individual student. Their eyes view a world framed in a first-person perspective. When they raise their hands in front of them, they do not see a person raising their hands—they only see their own hands being raised. When they throw a ball, they do not feel the ball being caught by the other person's hands, they only see the ball being caught and thrown back to them. When we ask students to consider the point of view of another person, or the author of a book, we are asking students to imagine viewing information from the first-person perspective of another human.

Perspective is a cognitive task that develops in the earliest of elementary grade levels. An example of this development has been shown in studies involving students viewing a model of a mountain. These students are then shown the same model of a mountain from a different perspective and may or may not recognize that mountain depending on the perspective they were originally shown. This is similar to the idea of constellations that have been proven to only exist due to our location in our own universe and that if we were to travel to a different location in our universe those same constellations would no longer exist—from our new perspective. It is this challenge of developing perspective in our students that we, as teachers, must first understand in ourselves and with each other well enough to describe this power of perspective in ways that a young human may begin to conceptually understand and develop in themselves.

Empathy in the Classroom

Empathy becomes crucial when approaching classroom management. When a student misbehaves, consider whether that student has developed a sense of empathy that would allow them to understand their effect on other students. Oftentimes, we as teachers want to punish students for interrupting our instruction or disturbing a positive learning environment with what is deemed as *bad* behavior. It is important to remember that, when a student disrupts the learning of others, it is not about that disruptive student being *bad*—it's about the other students who are no longer learning. It is important to teach all students to recognize the value of what is being taken away from them when a student disrupts the class. In those moments of disruption, it is important to remind the class how their success is dependent on the behavior of others, that the responsibility for learning is shared between all of us, and that it is okay to politely remind disruptive students that it is not the time or place for that behavior because they themselves want to improve.

This awareness takes a long time to instill in students who may have never experienced such ownership of learning. This idea of empathy in the classroom serves to develop in disruptive students an awareness that what they *want* in that moment is stopping others from what they *need*. With this practice, the idea of a teacher punishing a student for their behavior becomes a game that nobody wins if the students do not recognize the effect they are having on others. For those students who are rarely (if at all) disruptive in a classroom, it is equally important to instill in them the strength and resilience to speak out (respectfully) against disruptive students—cue those students and celebrate those moments when students are able to redirect each other for the benefit of all student learning in the classroom.

Interpersonal Skills

This fifth component is an area of social awareness and relationships that should not be age-referenced in its development since many interpersonal skills will develop at different rates for different students. Basic communication between humans differs between classrooms, schools, communities, states, and countries.

It is not the intention for this section to define which interpersonal skills are to be taught to students or at what age. The reader is encouraged to recognize and accept that development of cultures around the globe may not agree with particular examples in this section and that the purpose of this section is to allow readers to identify and develop skills with intention according to the intended outcomes of their school and community.

Basic interpersonal skills may begin with students knowing how to say *please* and *thank you*, understanding why we share and take turns, saying *no* when it is unsafe, and learning appropriate ways to welcome yourself to a group conversation. However, interpersonal skills become more socially divided as they get more complex. For example, nondefensive responses to criticism and accusation can be difficult to learn through experience alone—specific instruction may need to be provided for students at some point in their development of these skills. The idea of altruism (unrewarded kindness toward others) as a strategic response to aggression is not always automatically known by students. As students get older, these skills may require instruction, coaching, guidance, and in some cases role-playing in the classroom to prepare for social interactions motivated by one emotion or another.

For this reason, one could say that interpersonal skills are the catalyst of social and emotional learning, linking self-awareness and management to social awareness and relationships. The outward communication toward others of the coping strategies learned when dealing with compound and complex emotions could all fall under the area of interpersonal skills, but the benefit is in how each connect with the interpersonal skills to be developed for each purpose. For example, when an older student begins to feel themselves falling into a power imbalance with another person and learns to recognize the effects of such an outside negative influence on their self-esteem and behavior, the need to identify whether to scrap or salvage such relationships will require strong interpersonal communication skills.

These interpersonal skill sets develop even deeper into high school age groups. For example, the recognition and communication between certain leadership styles requires both the use and the interpretation of certain words and phrases to ensure each person understands the other. Another example is the ability to identify merit in content separate from the individual sharing the content. This area of social awareness and relationships is a key component to a person's ability to work alongside others and create positive and productive relationships.

Conflict Resolution

This sixth component is an ongoing life skill that can begin at the earliest elementary grade levels. Humans experience conflict at all stages of life. Even at these early elementary levels, students can begin recognizing constructive versus destructive ways to deal with conflict. The earlier that we expect students to discuss and practice conflict de-escalation strategies and techniques (e.g., self-calming, anger management), the better prepared they will be when more complex emotions and situations arise.

Students beginning their conversation on conflict resolution may need to begin with identifying examples of conflict to help build an understanding of conflict as a disagreement. Describing *constructive* versus *destructive* strategies for resolving conflict can begin with simple problems that arise in every day student life. Introducing coping strategies into daily classroom practice and modeling how positive self-talk can help relieve tension and ease conflict would be great at the beginning stages of this development.

With each grade level, students will experience various degrees of conflict in the form of wanting something and not receiving what they want. This will become especially true as peer pressure begins to take hold at home and at school. Including conflict resolution into classroom instruction can provide students opportunities to identify conflict and be prepared when others attempt to resolve the conflict unfairly. Students benefit from being taught to identify behaviors in their peers that are unhealthy or are causing unhealthy reactions in others. Being able to describe these paths toward conflict resolution will empower students to recognize their own value and determine whether a solution is, in fact, fair for all involved.

Types of Conflict

Disagreements (conflicts) will occur between students, parents, teachers, staff, and administration. Being able to recognize conflicts that are passive, assertive, or aggressive is an important awareness to develop in students.

Passive conflicts such as silence, passing notes, or avoidance may not always be clearly observable when they start and may not even require immediate resolution. The adage, *time heals all wounds,* may be applied to small conflicts through temporary avoidance but, as teachers, our role is to identify and monitor these kinds of conflicts to ensure resolution occurs. Two friends observed not talking to each other for a day or two that, the next day, are suddenly seen spending time together again may only require a teacher to kindly inquire what happened between the two friends. However, a small group of three or four close friends that have suddenly broken off into three or four separate groups may require some inquiry into how things are going in that small group. It may not be anything more than those friends taking a break from each other and finding joy in the company of other students, or perhaps a minor misunderstanding that can be resolved through a brief group chat. The point is that passive conflicts, when identified, can be resolved before they are misinterpreted and escalate into an aggressive verbal or physical conflict.

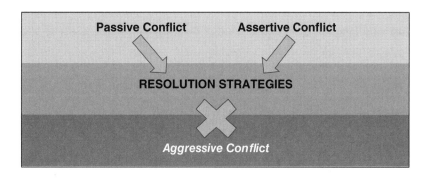

Assertive conflicts can be emotional reactions to a misunderstanding that requires immediate intervention to avoid escalation. This type of assertive conflict is easily observable as it is happening and students can be taught to recognize and apply de-escalation techniques for these types of conflicts, though it may be necessary for a teacher or other authority on campus to intervene. Assertive conflicts can also be intentional cause-and-effect confrontations. This can be the case when a student is learning to stand up for themselves, to defend themselves, and to identify themselves as a person unwilling to be taken advantage of, and they may do so by addressing others with an assertive tone. This can be difficult for teachers to mediate as we often promote our students to be assertive. The point at which mediation may be necessary is when the reaction to such assertive conflict is received with emotional reactions that can result in aggressive conflict escalation.

Strategies for Resolution

Students in elementary grade levels can develop emotional coping strategies and be able to identify basic conflict resolution techniques. By their middle school years, it will be important to consider more complex logic-based conflict resolution strategies. For example, the Flood-Dresher experiment is a win-win resolution strategy that considers scenarios where all individuals involved in the conflict or disagreement technically gain to some degree, even though some will be receiving less than others. It is important to play out scenarios in classroom environments to allow students to think through these types of conflicts and discuss how a win-win resolution isn't always equal but provide the best possible gains compared to other solutions.

It is also important to recognize that direct instruction on the benefits of conflict resolution strategies may not be enough for students to internalize these practices. It will be equally important for some students to experience these conflicts and, when the conflict is resolved for better or for worse, discuss resolution strategies for deeper reflection of the emotional impact. Although such an active approach to learning about conflict resolution can be effective, it can also be effective to take a preventative approach by preparing students to recognize and mediate conflicts as they witness them happening. The following strategies are not the only resolution strategies, nor are they to be considered the best, but are a few that I have had experience in teaching my own students in upper elementary and middle school.

RESOLUTION STRATEGY	BENEFITS
Scripts (Role-Play) in the Classroom Preventative Approach	Safe classroom environment
	Practice using "I" statements
	Explore different situations and contexts
	Discuss roles/responsibilities of observers

RESOLUTION STRATEGY	BENEFITS
Private Conversation **Active Approach**	Removes instigation from observers
	Removes some need for defensive reactions
	Promotes honesty between those involved
Active Listening **Active Approach**	Avoids sarcasm
	Appropriate eye contact
	Promotes restating what the other says
Benevolence/Altruism **Preventative and Active Approach**	Recognizes *need* in others
	Considers *importance* of conflict in context
	Promotes giving what is available to give

As students' abilities to identify and resolve conflict evolve, students will naturally seek to de-escalate conflict as it arises. Describing strategies and techniques for de-escalation management will look different at different grade levels—it is important for us as teachers to recognize what students are likely ready to implement. Through our daily observation, we may see how some students are exercising certain tones in their voice, controlling their body language, recognizing early aggressive signs in others, or kindly offering positive alternative activities to a peer's negative suggestions. When we as teachers are equipped to recognize what our students are ready to handle, we will be better suited to support this development in our students and celebrate their healthy and positive relationships with others.

SOCIETAL RESPONSIBILITY

The Collaborative for Academic, Social, and Emotional Learning (CASEL) connects responsible decision making with ethical standards, safety concerns, and social norms. This CASEL competency promotes identifying and analyzing situations in ways that develop an awareness of ethical responsibility for oneself and others. The two components related to this area in this book's approach to societal awareness combines and reorganizes these CASEL competencies into two components: Responsibility (Rules and Consequences) and Caring and Citizenship (Community Building).

Responsibility (Rules and Consequences)

This seventh component is intended to incorporate broad worldviews including short- and long-range effects of a student's own behavior. The idea that a student's actions have consequences beyond what students can see is a concept that takes time to develop. The ability to connect classroom rules and consequences with school-wide communities, eventually connecting to state and global issues, creates in students a broader sense and purpose of their own self-awareness and management.

The beginning stages of this component are focused more on rules and boundaries at school, at home, and, with a limited perspective, a student's community. The idea behind this early stage of development connects with the values that are taught in recognizing helpful community services and people such as police, firefighters, teachers, and doctors. As students move through the elementary grade levels, their worldview will likely be more concrete in their understanding of rules and consequences. A concrete example of an expanding worldview at the upper elementary grade levels could be participating in a community program that assists others in need such as helping with a weekend food drive at their school or volunteering with their family at a local homeless shelter. Later stages develop more abstract ideas of effects (consequences) on a broader stage that includes larger community, state, and national topics. As students develop through middle and high school grade levels, this awareness can develop into a more global worldview that might cause a school's framework of values to be put into contexts that challenge that of a student's own personal beliefs, lifestyle, and community involvement. This developing awareness and interest in community outreach efforts and increase in concern over national and global issues is the connecting tissue for abstract ideas of ethics and principals of both local and global consequences.

Media influence is a large part of societal responsibility as students develop an awareness of social norms and expectations beyond that of their school. These opportunities to develop a stronger sense of identity and self-efficacy in students, especially in the middle and high school grade levels, influence student identity and self-efficacy. The ability to express feelings amongst each other regarding media expectations at these older grade levels is an important skill to develop. This may include techniques, purposes, and reasoning behind propaganda, marketing, and advertising of ideas as well as products. As students get older, their conversations may include ethical considerations about the responsibility of our actions on communities, both locally and globally.

Caring and Citizenship (Community Building)

This eighth component is intended to develop a community awareness and improvement through individual and group engagement. There are various tiers of responsibility within any size community that work for and with each other. Local communities have groups and committees that work together to provide support services and events. Larger communities at the city and state level have government bureaucracies that manage various tiers of public service.

A student is introduced to these ideas in early elementary grade levels by helping at home and in the classroom to make things easier for themselves and others. Students can expand on this by identifying needs at home and in the classroom, even writing letters to a school leader suggesting possible ways to help. By providing classroom jobs, and supporting students in efforts to join school groups, this sense of community becomes more internalized.

As students enter middle and high school grade levels, the desire to help plan and eventually lead an effort to improve a community will begin with a student's school or surrounding community. Learning to research and delegate as part of a leadership role is inherent in this awareness as students either lead or follow with the intention to improve their own community. For some teachers, this may serve personal interests for activism of particular issues locally or globally. It is important to provide guidance and model for students how a person can become involved in helping to solve issues that are important to them. In the younger grade levels, a teacher may lead their whole class in a particular activity or project that addresses a specific issue. As students get older, their own interests may be served as the class decides which issues they wish to address as a class project. In the oldest grade levels, individual and small group projects may be supported as students are prompted and encouraged to participate in community events. These projects can incorporate academic standards through oral or written presentations of involvement and project conclusions. What is important to note here is that the combination of goal-setting, interpersonal skills, empathetic reasoning, and conflict resolution strategies that become involved in community improvement projects makes this aspect of community building a culminating area of social and emotional learning.

This culminating feature is one that a school may address together as part of a vision that can be backward designed to align grade-level projects or provide resources and networks for developing student-led projects. It is this part of this eighth component that is less about developing skills and more about developing a global worldview throughout the years a student experiences projects across the grade levels.

CHAPTER 3

Cognitive and Psychosocial Human Development

At the schools I have worked, I often connected with the special education team to discuss and reaffirm certain inclusive aspects of my classroom management approach. It is important to always learn more about how students develop cognitively at various rates and, as it has been shown in numerous studies (and traditionally accepted theories), not all students work through cognitive stages in the same pattern of intra-stage development.

While there are many theorists that have offered numerous perspectives on cognitive and psychosocial development, the following are overviews of only a few theorists on which I have chosen to base my own approach.

COGNITIVE HUMAN DEVELOPMENT

Jean Piaget

Jean Piaget (1896–1980) is commonly referred to as the grandfather of cognitive development. His theory of cognitive development introduces four stages: sensorimotor stage (birth to around two years), preoperational stage (around two years up through early childhood), concrete-operational stage (early childhood through adolescence), and formal-operational stage (adolescence through adult).

PIAGET'S THEORY OF COGNITIVE DEVELOPMENT		
Birth–2 years	Sensorimotor	Develops senses and motor skills; learns to use items; object permanence
2–6 years	Preoperational	Symbolic thinking and language; egocentric thought processing; conservation develops
7–11 years	Concrete Operational	Abstract concepts understood through concrete examples (time, space, etc.)
12–Adult	Formal Operational	Theoretical, abstract, hypothetical concepts (ethics, politics, nuance, etc.)

These stages may refer to general age ranges, but it is important to note that the age ranges of each stage are not subject to stopping and starting at a specific age. Rather, Piaget himself refers to these stages with phrases such as "after the age of 7–8" and "about the age of 11–12" (Piaget, 1928, p. 244). For the classroom teacher, this means that the group of students in a second- or third-grade classroom (around ages seven to eight) may have students at various degrees of cognitive transition. The same goes for classroom teachers of middle school grade levels (around ages eleven to twelve). Recognizing the individual student's transition through these cognitive stages is a critical aspect of understanding human development, especially when it comes to managing a classroom full of young humans expected to learn a prescribed set of concepts and skills.

Robbie Case

The past few decades have seen a revival of Piaget's work in the form of various critiques toward his theories; these are often referred to as Neo-Piagetian schools of thought. One critique in particular is a perspective from cognitive theorist Robbie Case (1944–2000). He not only proposes Executive Control Stages that correspond to Piaget's stages, he also proposes steps that attempt to explain differences of cognitive development in individual people. To do this, he describes a complexity sequence as a subset of developmental stages.

CASE'S COMPLEXITY SEQUENCE AS IT CORRESPONDS TO PIAGET'S COGNITIVE DEVELOPMENT THEORY		
Birth–2 years	Sensorimotor	Develops senses and motor skills; awareness of action-reaction relationships
2–5 years	Inter-Relational	Coordinates two inter-relational structures that are qualitatively different

CASE'S COMPLEXITY SEQUENCE AS IT CORRESPONDS TO PIAGET'S COGNITIVE DEVELOPMENT THEORY		
6–11 years	Dimensional	Coordinates conceptual structures and inter-relationship functions for causation
12–Adult	Vectorial	Extends understanding of relationships between two or more dimensions, or factors, of concepts.

For example, in Chapter 13 of Case's book, *The Mind's Staircase* (1991), he examines "the changes that take place in children's drawing during the period from 4 to 10 years of age" (p. 230) for which children ages four, six, eight, and ten are asked to draw specific scenes. His results and discussions hypothesize that "for the ages examined, there is a parallel between children's performance in drawing a picture and in other problem-solving tasks." (p. 237) Because this age range includes the transition of Piaget's preoperational to concrete-operational stages, it is important to note how Case's discussion of the children's drawings correspond to the transition of Piaget's stages. The drawings in Case's study by students who fall into Piaget's preoperational stage, ages four and six respectively, were primarily simple foreground drawings which are limited to a few elements of dots, lines, circles, and the like. While a higher level of organization is found in the age six drawings compared to the age four drawings, the change in drawings from age six to age eight includes depth that separates the foreground focus and the background scene. The age ten drawings add a middle ground which provides more complexity to their drawings not seen in earlier ages.

Case labels this sequence of developmental steps as (1) operational consolidation, (2) operational coordination, (3) bifocal coordination, and (4) elaborated coordination.

CASE'S DEVELOPMENTAL STAGES	
Step 1: Operational Consolidation	Assimilate general structure of new concept or skill
Step 2: Operational/ Unifocal Coordination	Apply new concept or skill to a single factor
Step 3: Bifocal Coordination	Able to focus a concept or skill on two factors at a time
Step 4: Elaborated Coordination	Extend new concept or skill to a variety of factors

Research of Piaget and Case has shaped my perspective toward differentiating and scaffolding my instruction of both academic and social aspects of human development. For any particular skill that may be new to a student, I must first recognize the need to assimilate a skill in a general sense (*operational consolidation*) which can then be followed by a development of coordinating factors such as quantity, quality, space, or organization (*operational coordination*) where each factor is individually addressed. At this point, it can be expected that two factors can be applied (*bifocal coordination*) until, finally, a child can be expected to apply multiple coinciding factors (*elaborated coordination*).

Case connects this development of inter-stage cognitive task to the development of working memory and, in his example of children's drawings, a child's ability to store increasing numbers of intentionally drawn objects and layers with increasing complexity. However, for me, I see Case's drawing exercise as a cross-reference for Piaget's transition between stages from pre-operational to concrete operational. This helps me to understand how students in grade levels corresponding to their age, especially when involving a particular transition (in this case the transition around ages six to eight), will see variability in student problem solving when it comes to tasks involving increasing complexity.

One aspect of Case's example that I like most is the idea that any inter- or intra-stage cognitive transition may be viewed through his complexity sequence. Understanding his idea on assimilating, coordinating, and elaborating with regard to cognitive development helps me to understand how to address a particular student transitioning between or through a Piagetian stage in order to develop that student's ability to master a specific concept or skill.

In practice, I use this insight into human cognitive development to shape my perspective toward academic expectations. Not every child in first grade (around age 6) will be ready to draw, or problem solve, to the same degree of complexity as their peers. Instead, I must remember to provide instructional opportunities for each child to develop and acquire an increasing degree of complexity that meets the developmental needs of each student. This example supports the idea that my instruction guides student development while simultaneously allowing student development to cue my instruction. It is then critical that I am aware of and able to identify the development of each child as they succeed in developing the cognitive capacity for mastering new concepts and skills.

For example, a third grader (around age 8) may be expected to reach the following end goal: *provide evidence to support a statement regarding a story's central idea.*

This requires multiple points of detail to be coordinated strategically in order to provide reasonable support for a claim. If I apply Case's complexity sequence (assimilate, coordinate, elaborate), I may relate this student's initial effort in writing general information about the story to Cage's basic *operational consolidation* of a concept or skill which, for a child at this age and grade level, may be considered behind that which is expected. However, in identifying this cognitive sequence, I may offer that student an opportunity to work toward the level of *operational coordination* by requiring the student to resubmit their work focusing only on one aspect of the end goal. As the student masters each individual factor with each resubmission of their work, I am developing in that student an awareness of academic expectation, one factor at a time, and will eventually require the student to resubmit a final sample that highlights two or more aspects of the end goal for a proficient score. Through practice and self-reflection, the student will eventually get to the point where their initial submissions provide relevant evidence to support a statement regarding a story's central idea.

In addition to this example, since this third grader is around the age where they may possibly still be transitioning from Piaget's stages of preoperational to concrete operational, I can also consider starting this sequence of cognitive development with more playful and fictional topics and stories of personal interest as the student is guided through this concept or providing evidence for their statements. Again, this is an example of how instruction guides development while simultaneously allowing student development to cue my instruction.

PSYCHOSOCIAL HUMAN DEVELOPMENT

Erik Erikson

Erik Erikson (1902–1994) developed a popular framework for human psychosocial development that includes eight stages he called the "eight ages of man" (Erikson, 1966). All eight stages of his framework target specific aspects of self and social human development from birth to death, but I feel it is important for me as a teacher to focus on the first six of the eight stages as they span from birth to young adulthood which covers the years from birth to kindergarten all the way up to the years just after high school.

Erikson's stages are often referred to as *crises*, or traumatic upheavals, but, as a teacher, it may be better to view these stages as increasingly complex explorations with no distinct beginning or end. While this makes it difficult to match expected behaviors to specific ages, it is important to consider the idea that while each stage may begin *around* a suggested age, no stage actually stops developing. This is important because any crisis at an early age that develops negatively may have compounded effects on later stages. As a teacher, I find this incredibly important in identifying in my students the social and emotional behaviors that may or may not be rooted in a particular event or reaction on any given day. The behaviors of a student I observe may not represent their personality as it will always be; what I'm observing may be a reaction to an experience that is learned through past experiences that have taught them to cope with a particular strategy of comedy, indifference, or disdain. This can be true at nearly any age and how we communicate to a person about their reactions at different stages will depend on their age, the stage, and the person's cognitive ability to rationalize and self-reflect.

Erikson's *eight stages* begins from birth to about 18 months and focuses on a *Trust versus Mistrust* crisis which primarily involves feeding and developing a trusting relationship with a caregiver. As the child continues to gain more control over their body, they begin to explore the world around them which initiates a new crisis that focuses on things such as toilet training as they consider their own *Autonomy versus Shame/Doubt*. This stage is more about how they feel about themselves as opposed to how they feel about their actions. From around age three to age six, as the child becomes more assertive and explores their own independence, the child then begins to focus more on their *Initiative versus Guilt* with regard to how they feel about their actions. In the United States, a child begins school around age five, so a child may have had one or two years of school while possibly transitioning into a six-year crisis focusing on an idea of *Industry versus Inferiority* as they learn new skills and cope with failure in social settings. Adolescence is the term used to describe the next stage, beginning around age twelve, and focuses on peer relationships as they consider aspects of *Identity versus Role Confusion* with regard to gender roles, politics, religion, and other personal opinions about the world around them. It is common at this stage for students to begin feeling a separation between themselves and those that have been responsible for their well-being as they begin to create for themselves an identity of their own which can make their connections to peers, educators, and other role models outside of their family circles that much more important to their development throughout this stage. The sixth stage refers to a crisis occurring during *young adulthood* that focuses on *Intimacy versus Isolation* with regard to love relationships that can start near the end of high school and continue throughout a person's choices as they enter a college or career.

One aspect of Erikson's stages that must be included is the idea that a human can, later in life, revisit these stages with professional help and a coherent treatment strategy for psychological recovery. This is important to consider as an educator as I introduce this next section on development and a cognitive and psychosocial approach toward classroom instruction.

DEVELOPMENTAL MINDSET

Piaget, Case, and Erikson represent in my approach an awareness of student development that puts all students into a single inclusive model for instruction. I may never have a classroom with a group of students developing through the same developmental stages, at the same time, at the same rate. Therefore, when I consider my instructional approach, my traditional university training has me aiming for the median level of student ability—not advanced beyond a grade level, not remedial in cognition or psychosocial development, but differentiated for various student modes of learning within a set of specific age-based grade-level expectations. My developmental mindset takes this traditional approach toward teaching to the middle and works to widen the concept of differentiation to include all students at various levels of cognitive and psychosocial development.

This developmental mindset utilizes the theories of Piaget and Erikson, applying a complex scope of human development to students in my classroom. This mindset allows me to consider daily student actions and reactions as single events of a fluid development that spans beyond one academic school year. Whether I have students at age six, ten, or fourteen, the cognitive and psychosocial stages represented in the students assigned to me will differ causing each student's actions and reactions to be based on individual perspectives. This requires of me an awareness to identify and guide students through these compounding stages. It is this mindset that affords me the patience and understanding toward each student as I observe student behaviors throughout a single school year and discuss with previous teachers how their behaviors may be developing over time.

My instruction is also affected by cognitive stages. For example, an academic expectation may not be learned by a student because that student is not able to cognitively process the complexity of that skill. In this case, I may choose to wait until the student is developmentally ready to process that skill (through the instruction of other skills and developmental processing) at which point I can provide the resources and instruction for that student to move forward in their academic journey. This is different than choosing to present what is deemed as *age appropriate,* regardless of individual development, in an attempt to train that cognition to develop in the student. My developmental mindset considers how my instruction may guide development but it's the development that cues my instruction.

Developmental Transitions

As a teacher, I must recognize that students working through a transition period of two cognitive stages is important when determining how to manage a classroom. The response from students frustrated at being unable to cognitively grasp a task at a given complexity (perhaps required by grade-assigned academic standards) requires me to simultaneously consider the psychosocial aspect of their human development.

It's easy to get lost in the jargon of cognitive and psychosocial terminology. So, if you consider what each stage allows a child to do, it can be easier to keep your patience when a child may not be able to grasp a new academic concept. Consider the following graphic as a means for visualizing how these cognitive and psychosocial transitions overlap.

DEVELOPMENTAL TRANSITIONS		
COGNITIVE STAGES (PIAGET)	AGE	PSYCHOSOCIAL STAGES (ERIKSON)
	17	
	16	
	15	
	14	
	13	Identity vs. Role Confusion
Formal Operational	12	
	11	
	10	
	9	
	8	
	7	
Concrete Operational	6	Industry vs. Inferiority
	5	
	4	
Preoperational	3	Initiative vs. Guilt
	2	Autonomy vs. Shame
Sensorimotor	1	

Example: First Grade

A first-grade teacher may be assigned a classroom of students who are six years old at some point in the school year. **Cognitive Transition:** This means that these students will likely have developed through the cognitive *pre-operational* stage that includes abilities in symbolic thinking and language through egocentric thought processing while having developed general problem-solving skills. This also means that these students may be ready to develop into the cognitive *concrete-operational* abilities to understand concrete examples of abstract concepts. A first-grade teacher may consider the majority of first graders ready to learn about time, space, and quantity, so time may be taught with physical plastic clocks that students can manipulate and use as a visual aid to draw time on paper. That same teacher may consider students ready to learn about space by physically representing concepts of location and position (above, below, to the left of, etc.), and quantity through the practice of regrouping base ten blocks to show the concept of tens, hundreds, and thousands. **Psychosocial Transition:** It is equally important for teachers to practice patience and positivity during these years since students will have simultaneously entered a new psychosocial transition. Having already transitioned through the stage of

Autonomy vs Shame/Doubt (ages one to three) and Initiative vs Guilt (ages three to five), the stage of Industry vs Inferiority (ages five to twelve) will be a compounding factor for these students. This development will likely show itself through stronger desires to prove how industrious and successful they can be in relation to their peers. When you consider this

> *Instruction may be cueing cognitive developmental transitions while those developmental transitions may cue instruction.*

compounding transition for the majority of students in this grade level, it may become apparent how coping strategies (page 36) might help students learn to develop a healthy balance of competition and self-efficacy.

Example: Seventh Grade

A seventh-grade teacher may be assigned a classroom of students who are twelve years old at some point in the school year. **Cognitive Transition:** This means that these students will likely be amidst a transition from *concrete-operational* to *formal-operational* cognitive capacity that involves the beginnings of abstract and hypothetical reasoning (justice, complex emotions, nuance, nano-technologies, etc.). As a teacher, I must recognize that a group of students at or around age twelve may encompass a range of cognitive potential and must consider how assignments may fall within a range from heavily concrete to exceedingly abstract or hypothetical in their expectation of the student. Because these students may only be at the beginning of this transition, their hypothetical reasoning may seem weak or insufficient at first. **Psychosocial Transition:** It is also important to note that these students may also be in the process of entering into a new psychosocial development of *identity vs role confusion*. Through observations of behavior and student academic work samples, separating a student's cognitive development from their psychosocial development can help me consider ways to help a student master the expected academic skills in a way that meets their needs with an appropriate developmental mindset.

The first-grade and seventh-grade teachers are not the only grade-level teachers that will be affected by these transitions. The kindergarten and second-grade teachers will also see students developing through these stages, as will the fifth- through ninth-grade teachers. As for those teachers in between these transitions, it is important to recognize that a percentage of students entering their classrooms may not have had the support to help them through those transitions.

From these two examples, my developmental mindset can be adapted to meet the needs of students in most classrooms. Keep in mind that it likely isn't *the classroom* that can seem overwhelming to the teacher as much as the collection of each individual student's development to which other students may be reacting that becomes overwhelming. A developmental mindset will allow for development to play a key role in the academic and social-emotional instruction and intervention discussed in greater detail in part two of this book, secondary concepts.

SPECIAL EDUCATION

While cognitive and psychosocial development provides insight into a wide range of students entering classrooms, a percentage of students may fall into a different category of special education needs. This category is not completely separate yet not exactly the same when it comes to developmental patterns—there are a series of other considerations for which professionals in the special education world provide excellent insight.

My classrooms have always had *at least* one student with an Individualized Education Program (IEP), sometimes referred to as an Individualized Education Plan. This is typically developed by a team of specialists and school staff to identify specific needs for an individual student. My responsibilities, as a classroom teacher, for any student with an IEP is similar to any student in my classroom except for the specific legal document listing specific accommodations or modifications for an individual student.

When a student enters my classroom with an IEP, this student has already had their parents, previous teachers, administrators, and other education specialists discuss that student's ability to learn and have already agreed on the support services intended to meet that student's needs at the time of their last meeting. My role is to ensure that those support services are infused into my instruction and classroom management until the next IEP meeting where it can be determined if those support services are resulting in student success or if adjustments need to be made. I work closely with my special education team of professionals to ensure that my classroom is providing those specific support services for those students. If an accommodation or modification is unable to be met in my classroom, my role is to communicate with the special education team so a solution for meeting this student's support services can be met.

I have observed in the past students with an IEP in a traditional instructional model. In my experience, the support services in a student's IEP were listed in addition to the instructional plans. This is intended to specifically account for the required support services to be provided in the event an administrator or parent has any questions about a particular IEP. This was to ensure that all students are receiving effective instruction and behavior management specific to those students' needs. Something else I've also noticed in those traditional instructional models is that many of the accommodations specific to those students with IEPs are often intuitively implemented for students based on what the teacher observes on a daily basis. However, what I recognize as valuable for the IEP is the difference between what some teachers may do for students intuitively and what other teachers may need to intentionally remind themselves to do, especially when some students with an IEP may not have severely observable needs.

Shared Roles and Responsibilities

One thing that will be discussed in Chapter 6 is the idea that every student could benefit from particular accommodations and that the practice of incorporating those particular accommodations into the culture of a classroom serves to benefit all students, including those whose IEPs include those accommodations. This thought on special education, from my perspective as a general education classroom teacher, is based on an idea that no other students are so specifically assigned learning support services regardless of the benefits toward student learning. There is a percentage of students with IEPs that I have had enrolled in my classrooms over the years that do not require a one-on-one paraprofessional and whose accommodations include supportive strategies from which the majority of my students already benefit (preferential seating, restated directions, multiple prompting, etc.).

I recognize that a percentage of students with IEPs have specific accommodations and content modifications that address more severe needs than what I have described here—it is not these students who I am addressing at this point. This idea of shared roles and responsibilities is meant to consider the students with IEPs that include accommodations that overlap with the teaching strategies and general supports I may wish to provide to all of my students.

I consider this overlap of knowledge between myself as a general education classroom teacher and that of the special education professional as a shared role in educating all students. The depth of expertise in child development that the special education professionals have obtained provides a supportive structure that complements the strategies I utilize for my general education students. Students in my classes that are not officially and legally identified as needing special education services often benefit from the same strategies and targeted resources utilized by the special education professionals.

PART 2

Secondary Concepts

In Chapters 1–3, each of the three primary concepts were introduced. Chapters 4–6 will be looking at how each of the three *primary* concepts overlap to create *secondary* concepts.

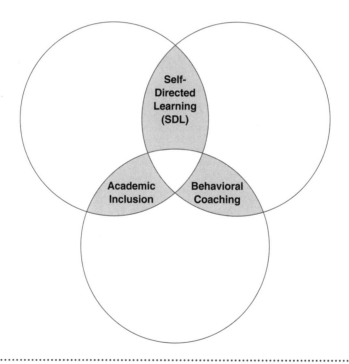

First, the standards-based academic learning and social-emotional learning concepts create a secondary concept: *Self-Directed Learning*. This is a classroom instructional approach that reframes academic instruction through a social-emotional lens and puts the classroom teacher in the position of an academic coach that facilitates learning more than a teacher whose primary role is to deliver direct instruction.

Second, the social-emotional learning and cognitive development concepts create a secondary concept: *Behavioral Coaching and Intervention*. This is an approach to student behavior management that supports all students, including those who may fall outside the range of general behavior expectations according to a school's framework for behavior. Chapter 5 is intentionally split into two parts to highlight the depth behind the single secondary concept of behavioral coaching and intervention. Since this secondary concept blends Social-Emotional Learning and Cognitive and Psychosocial Human Development, this two-part chapter looks at the interaction between the teacher and student relationship as well as the classroom and school environment. Part 1 of the chapter focuses more on how the teachers interact with their students in a classroom environment. Part 2 of the chapter focuses more on how the classroom environment interacts with the school-wide environment.

Third, cognitive and psychosocial development and standards-based learning concepts create a secondary concept: *Academic Inclusion and Intervention*. This looks at academic instruction that widens responsibilities for differentiation and classroom management to include all students who are both inside and outside the average range of academic progress across grade levels.

My experience in implementing these secondary concepts as a classroom teacher provides a limited perspective that may not serve as a model to be adopted without adaptation. The information presented regarding these ideas is meant to introduce my perspective and approach to concepts that have few textbooks on implementation.

CHAPTER 4

Self-Directed Learning

As I further prepare for the start of a new school year, I become excited thinking about how I am going to introduce my new students to the idea of Self-Directed Learning (SDL) and help to develop a new set of humans academically and behaviorally. As excited as I become, I must remember that this is almost always a new concept for students entering my classroom, especially in the elementary grade levels. Students are not used to the idea of being *self-directed* and may not understand the intention behind the phrase. In fact, a common interpretation from students when they first hear about this phrase is that I will want them to learn on their own. This interpretation, though false, is understandable. Traditionally, students look to me as their teacher to have all of the answers for each of their own sets of problems from day to day. When they have a question, they raise their hand to get an answer. When they have a concern, they raise their hand to ask me for a resolution. All questions and concerns are directed to me as *all-knowing* with an expectation that I will solve all classroom concerns. It can sometimes feel like students are carrying with them a *disentitlement* toward their own learning, an opposite of entitlement, that they are somehow not responsible for what or how they learn. Therefore, I must remember that when I introduce SDL that I am careful to slowly present pieces of this approach to learning a little bit at a time each week. The goal is to instill the idea of Self-Directed Learning as a collaborative approach that develops in students a sense of ownership over their own learning where I, as the *teacher*, merely provide the pathway by which students can guide themselves and each other to walk that provided path, coaching them in what and how to learn through transparent standards-based academic and social-emotional obstacles and expectations.

One thing about SDL is that it can exist outside of age-based and grade-level placement and, instead, focus on individual development of skills. The most important concept behind SDL is its *adaptability* for implementation with students of different ages and readiness. Early elementary students and middle school students will need to adapt differently to SDL to account for not only the academic expectations but also the social-emotional development to address the individual students in each classroom. As I introduce new academic ideas to my students, I will need to consider the language and context appropriate for their human development as learners. This requires me as the teacher to be aware of my own students' abilities and believe that my students are able to take ownership of their own learning, with guidance and support.

In its earliest adaptations, as a more *traditional* teacher begins to intentionally infuse concepts of Self-Directed Learning into their classroom, the focus may begin by targeting specific grade-level standards and age-based expectations to align with a school-wide or community-wide culture and perspective. To do this, the most important first step is shifting to a standards model of grading, assessment, and reporting, then adjusting a classroom's environment to account for the social-emotional development of individual students. As these primary concepts are infused, the Developmental Mindset in the third primary concept of human development widens a teacher's outlook on differentiation. This then allows the teacher to recognize the potential for learning of not just all but *each* of the students in a classroom by determining where a student is performing in any particular skill and providing instruction and support both academically and social-emotionally in a way that empowers that individual student to know success for themselves.

One mantra that I instill in my classroom that helps build a foundation for the ideas and aspects behind my approach to SDL is: *Watch. Listen. Think. Do. Explain.* Each word in this mantra develops in students a basis for learning about *learning styles* and helps them to recognize that people may prefer to watch, or listen, or do, but that a strength in a particular learning style is not the sole receptor for learning. In my classroom, this mantra helps to maximize the amount of input to the brain when learning and practicing by requiring all learning styles to be activated, regardless of student preference for one learning style over another. This is not a requirement for SDL but is rather an ongoing strategy, an adaptation, that I utilize prior to, and throughout, my own implementation of SDL.

In the following sections, I explain five aspects of Self-Directed Learning that I instruct new students throughout a school year to understand. There are various rates of progress based on individual ability in each of these five areas. I instruct students directly in each of the five areas over time starting at the beginning of the year. As students individually develop skill sets within each of the areas, my instruction of these areas becomes more customized to the shrinking group of students who require ongoing support. In this way, my guidance is ongoing for all students throughout the year.

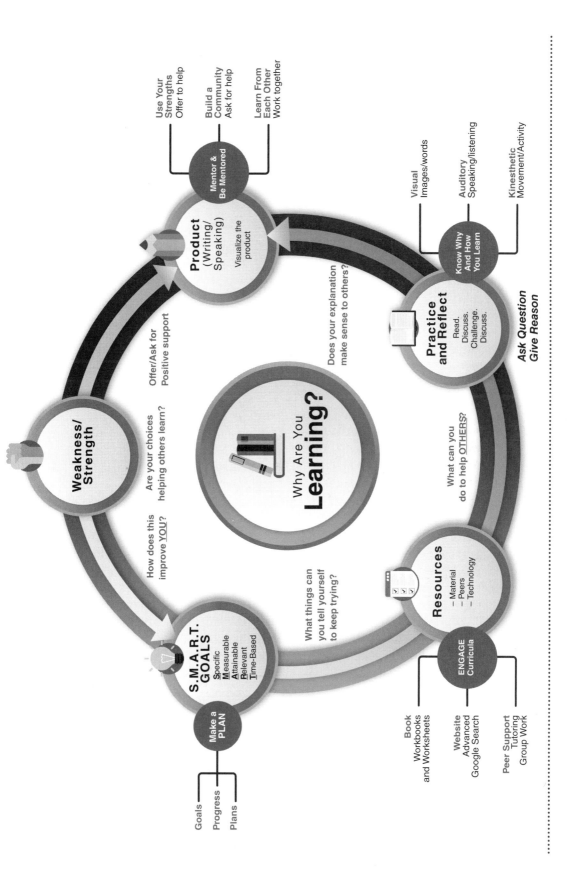

IDENTIFYING GROWTH VERSUS PROFICIENCY

This first area of Self-Directed Learning begins at the beginning of the school year, but not the first week of school. This area requires standards-specific student data that can be presented as information to students in a meaningful way. When I receive my student roster for the year, I typically seek specific information about what standards students mastered at the end of the prior school year. This tends to be an unfruitful endeavor, so I use the first week or so of school to gather that data. This provides me with the beginnings of my coaching students in identifying growth versus proficiency.

Connecting prior-year standards to current-year standards is covered in the Primary Concept of standards-based learning. Teacher mastery of standards requires me to understand how skills learned last year support skills to be taught this year; I am aware of those standards that may have concluded a particular skill last year as well as those that introduce new skills this year.

The first time I presented to my entire class this detailed standards-based information of their own academic progress, I was unsure how students would react. It wasn't until I explained the purpose of displaying this information that students began to recognize its value. Involving students in this first step of Self-Directed Learning is crucial, as it is this initial introduction that will naturally incorporate social-emotional learning components into the academic learning environment. As the classroom teacher, your role in guiding students through this initial phase of redefining student learning is paramount to the success of Self-Directed Learning.

During the first month or so of school, I am typically teaching academic skills from prior years and connecting them to very simplistic examples of current-year academic expectations. Since the academic expectations are not able to be assessed at the depth of cognitive complexity that may be required for every current-year academic standard, my grading and assessments of students are more about identifying in my students specific social-emotional learning components and what students are able to do with regard to self-awareness and management, social-awareness and relationships, and societal responsibilities. This information is not an objective assessment that is communicated to students and parents but rather utilized in my own adjustment of academic and behavior management.

Students are shown how they can master any skill when provided tasks at various levels of cognitive complexity. Clearly, a kindergarten or first grade student might not understand what that means but they would recognize and communicate confidence in their ability to complete a task similar to that of his or her peers. As explained in the Primary Concept of cognitive development, students at these youngest elementary ages have entered Erikson's psychosocial stage of Industry versus Inferiority. These youngest students may not need to understand the abstract inner-workings of the differentiated tasks being provided; they may only need to know that they can master each skill alongside their peers. As the teacher, notating at what depth of complexity each student can master each skill will be important as each student progresses through the grade levels. For an older student at the upper elementary or middle school age range, introducing such abstract inner workings of cognitive complexity may be understood with assistance from a concrete model of learning as they progress throughout the school year. I personally use a wall chart in my classroom that shows not only the academic standards expected to be mastered by the end of that school year but differentiated colors that represent each level of cognitive complexity. I then label each standard on the wall chart with each standard's expected level of complexity according to the grade level standards I have been assigned to teach. These levels are explained in more detail in the Primary Concept of standards-based learning (see Defining Proficiency).

As students are introduced to their progress of individual standards, there are a series of social-emotional developments that occur as students either recognize that they are not mastering certain skills that have been mastered by others or that they are among the few that are mastering so many more standards than others. These are the crucial moments that make my job as the classroom teacher so vital to this particular area of Self-Directed Learning.

First is the focus toward students' Self-Awareness and Management, specifically Self-Efficacy and Improvement. Although the conversation is rooted in a student's ability to identify and manage their own feelings and emotions, the target in this context is the student's ability to identify value in *growth* rather than *proficiency*. Assisting the class in evaluating these two words, specifically in those moments when students are experiencing self-doubt, it is in these experiences that students can feel the empowerment of growth *as a path toward* proficiency. This conversation also lends itself well to the social-emotional idea of Self-Reflection and Goal-Setting as you use your own understanding as a professional educator to explain how *growth* can be like grass that wants to grow—you can't expect to grow overnight and, if it still isn't growing, then consider improving the environment of the grass. Any metaphor can be challenged by pointing out inconsistent comparisons of the two ideas being compared, and this may be expected from students who feel they are not growing. As the teacher, I know which skills a student has already mastered in various subjects and can quickly shift the conversation to this student's strengths to make the point that they are capable of mastering skills and that it takes time, practice, patience, practice (because it can take twice as much practice), and when it still seems difficult, practice in a different way the next day, but to never give up. To help the student focus on this idea of persistence, or *grit* as some call it, it is helpful to refer to a goal-setting strategy such as a SMART Goals to help students keep a timeline of their effort and success. SMART Goals are discussed in more detail in the Standards-Based Learning section of this book under Self-Reflection and Goal-Setting (page 39). Whatever strategy you choose to adapt in your classroom would be a fitting tool to meet the needs of a student working through this social-emotional aspect of academic success.

Next is the focus toward students' Social-Awareness and Relationships, specifically Empathy and Perspective. This will almost always be a class discussion. Even when the impetus is a specific student or very small group of students, this conversation must be one in which all students are involved. Students likely have concerns similar to any other student struggling with a skill or idea. Especially in the K–8 grade levels, accessing this inherent psychosocial desire for industriousness through either academic or social constructs provides ample opportunities for discussion of empathy and perspective. By recognizing that all students in the classroom have yet to master something is not to highlight what students *can't* do but is meant rather to highlight what students have *yet* to do—the idea of *growth* over *proficiency*. When this idea is discussed as a class, students' interpersonal skills can be guided to support empathetic reasoning. While telling students to support each other through empathy may be received as a command, offering students repeated examples of the growth students have made in specific skills and the progress they are making with support by either me as their teacher or other students will provide students the necessary opportunities to internalize the concept of empathy. This brings the conversation back to the idea that all students inherently have similar concerns as their peers, similar to any other student struggling with a specific skill or idea, and that it is the support of their peers, family, and community that will make a much larger impact on an individual student's success.

Finally, and this is not always included in ongoing conversations but does have quite a powerful effect when internalized by a large number of students, are the effects of supporting one another on the overall strength and effectiveness of the school as a positive learning environment. One example of this aspect of the conversation focused on student self-efficacy, improvement, empathy, and perspective is the larger idea how wishing for a school to be a safe place to be requires students to be the kinds of people that make that school a safe place to be, and that wanting a school to be a respectful place to be requires students to be the kinds of people that make that school a respectful place to be. This idea gets even larger when students begin to consider that a classroom of students who learn to be Self-Directed Learners must then recognize that all other classrooms that may not be self-directed may not share these values of safety and respect outside of their own classrooms. It is therefore up to those of us that understand and value these ideas to help those around us. This idea seeds the beginnings of societal responsibility and community building, planted in the safety of the student's classroom where the idea can be shared and practiced daily out on the yard, at lunch, and even between classes.

All of this is part of the combined standards-based learning and social-emotional learning I refer to as Self-Directed Learning. It takes time for these ideas to take hold in the classroom and be instilled in the hearts and minds of your students, especially the first year that they are introduced. At the core of these ideas is myself as the teacher that not only must instruct and guide these ideas throughout the school year but also model these expected actions and reactions on a daily basis.

MAKE A PLAN (SMART GOALS)

This second area of Self-Directed Learning is subtle and more long term. My role in this area is to develop in students a recognition of their own growth and progress through which their own growth is monitored. It is a daily effort to ensure all students are consciously tracking progress toward reaching daily, weekly, and monthly goals. The challenge is figuring out how each student best responds to goal-tracking strategies. Some students will respond well to journals and logs. Others will need a more visible tactile approach such as desktop or wall trackers that can then be transcribed weekly—with ease. Still some will struggle with just the idea of writing down a goal; these students will have the hardest time with this area and may need the most guidance and oversight. Above all else is the challenge in avoiding the simplest solution for this expectation simply out of indifference and, instead, discovering the value of goal-setting and identifying tasks and strategies that the student acknowledges are responsible for their learning.

As the classroom teacher, my duty in helping all students learn to plan and track their progress requires patience and leniency. When students are not succeeding, it is good to consider offering those students opportunities to either consider a goal-setting strategy or revise the strategy they are using.

I will often start students with the SMART Goals strategy since it specifies helpful parameters for goal-setting. SMART goals are: Specific, Measurable, Attainable, Relevant, and Time-Based. Other teachers will have their own preference for starting students out with a goal-setting strategy. Allowing students opportunities to choose a different strategy rather than forcing a teacher-preferred strategy is important in helping students see the value and ownership in their own learning. Students who do not adopt or adapt a goal-setting strategy are not reprimanded or punished but as certain skills are difficult, I may ask them how often they have attempted that skill. Without a goal-setting and self-reflection strategy to track their progress, they become aware of the difficulty remembering all of the tasks they attempt over long periods of time. This discussion point is had many times with these students throughout the school year. It has been my experience that at least a few students do not ever take to a goal-setting strategy and still manage to master enough academic standards to move on to the next grade level.

Another means for tracking growth and progress is something I call *Standard Notes*. These notes encompass all five areas of self-directed learning but, at this second stage, focuses on writing down exactly what standard and skill is being learned and providing specific lessons in a textbook or website that addresses the specific standard or skill. Taking the time to write down the standard and skill, the objective, and the related tasks helps students to review what they have learned over time which eventually turns into a journal-like notebook of learning. This can then be reviewed whenever a student may have forgotten a skill or is being asked by a peer to assist in their learning.

SELF-DIRECTED GOAL-SETTING NOTES

Use these guiding questions to help you reflect on your progress.

1 – Skill/Standard

What exactly are you learning? _____

_____

What is your objective, or goal? _____

_____

2 – Tasks

What will you do to practice that skill/standard? _____

_____

How will you know when you have completed each task? _____

_____

3 – Resources

What will you use to help you with your task? _____

_____

How are you using that resource to help you learn? _____

_____

4 – Strategies

How will you use your resources to overcome obstacles? _____

_____

When a task gets difficult, what strategy can help you practice? ___

_____

5 – Product

What will you show to prove you are progressing? _____

_____

What level of proficiency does your product meet? _____

_____

The purpose of a goal-setting strategy is to train students in selecting a specific skill or standard and identify what tasks are most appropriate for that skill or standard. The task a student chooses may very well be a task that you as the teacher have included in your direct instruction of that skill. The task may also be out of a textbook, from a website, or other means of guidance. As long as the student can describe the task and how it is targeting the skill or standard as part of their goal, the goal-setting strategy, as it applies to this second area of Self-Directed Learning, is working.

Standards-Based Learning (Assessments) is a big component of this aspect of self-directed learning as it is a much clearer example of how standards-based academics can overlap with social-emotional development. Earlier in this book, I talk about how formative assessments gauge learning over time and I give examples for not reporting grades on formative tasks. In this current section, it is therefore important to take that idea further. Formative tasks can provide profound and lasting influence on a student's social and emotional development and the affect these tasks have on academic learning is to be seen as merely an effect of what is actually being taught—ongoing goal-setting and self-reflection.

Self-Reflection is a developing aspect of this area of Self-Directed Learning as students begin to realize that they must set realistic goals that benefit them over time. Many of my own students begin with arbitrary goals they are able to accomplish quickly. This leaves those students feeling unsatisfied in goal-setting as a concept because they have not internalized its value. As students use goal-setting strategy journals and logs to set a goal and track their progress, they will need guidance in self-reflection to recognize their own reactions to what is ultimately their own decision-making process. It may take some students longer to recognize their own patterns of inconsistent practice and relate that to a skill that is not improving. This becomes more difficult when other students don't seem to practice some skills and are able to master them anyway. My role of the classroom teacher at this point is to maintain consistent oversight of student goal-setting and provide opportunities for students to practice reflecting in their own words:

1. What skills needed more or less practice?
2. What tasks were more helpful in mastering different skills?
3. For skills that were not mastered at a level of proficiency desired, what other tasks might help you master those skills?

It is important to note here that early elementary grade levels will likely require the teacher to model this goal-setting strategy for students throughout the school year and may modify the self-reflective aspects to account for attention and cognitive complexity. Students in the upper elementary grade levels will be more open to managing their own goal-setting strategies but may need consistent modeling by the teacher as they develop these increasingly complex skills. It is when students reach middle and high school grade levels, even those that are new to goal-setting, that they may be held accountable by their teachers on a daily or weekly basis with self-reflective entries to challenge their development as learners. Over time, students can begin to internalize these aspects of Self-Directed Learning and are able to monitor their own progress effectively. The earlier that students get to witness and experience this process of improving as a self-directed learner, the more accustomed they become to the benefits of making a plan, goal-setting, and self-reflection.

RESOURCES

The third area of Self-Directed Learning has to do with the resources that students are provided as self-directed learners. Resources may include manipulatives and measurement tools for math or science, documents and artifacts for history, social science, or language arts, and specific books or websites that can be accessed for any topic. Even a peer or tutor that has knowledge of content and strategies for a topic can be a resource. This section will go over both the teacher and student roles for developing self-directed learners as it applies to student self-discipline and integrity as a self-directed learner.

Right off the bat, I will say that misuse or neglect of a resource is a daily struggle for teachers and, while this problem is simple to identify, it is a difficult problem to resolve, especially when it comes to students using classroom resources independently as self-directed learners.

When I am provided with a resource without instruction, I will likely neglect, minimally use, or creatively use that resource in ways other than originally intended. Although these resources may become useful to me to varying degrees, their value may be undercut, and I may be underserved due to my own misunderstanding or misuse of a resource. When I receive computer software, math manipulatives, artifacts, and other materials, these resources will require a level of instruction, discovery, and practice before I am ready to use these in an instructional environment. As a teacher, the depth of mastery that I will want to have of each resource will need to account for the varying needs of any student who walks into my classroom.

Like teachers, when students are provided a resource without instruction, they may neglect, minimally use, or creatively use that resource in much the same way a teacher might in a similar situation. The biggest difference between a student and a teacher misusing a resource is the life experiences that can help make sense of a resource in various ways. As a teacher (even as just an adult), I may have seen a resource used a different way or have seen some similar resource used in a way that may be applicable. Likewise, students may have seen a resource used a different way or can visualize in their mind's eye a way that resource may be used. However, students may not have this life experience to support such an open approach to using resources. Students experiencing a resource for the first time may need consistent coaching to ensure that a resource is being used productively (or simply as a nondistraction).

This awareness of the similarity between how I and my students may assimilate and adapt resources based on our past life experience and associations allows me the leniency, but also the foresight, to consistently coach students in using resources throughout the year. Some students will be ready to use resources independently (with a focused intent for learning) early on, while some students will need long-term coaching before they can be expected to utilize various resources with focused intent for learning. This is the third area of Self-Directed Learning because it requires a student to know which resources best provide support for their plan of completing learning tasks that target specific growth of particular skills or standards.

Grade Level Expectations for Resources

This is a great place in this section to recognize that early elementary students can be self-directed learners within a controlled schedule for learning and clear visual signals for actions and direction. Upper elementary students are definitely able to be self-directed learners within a controlled schedule for learning as they become more solidified in an increasingly concrete logic-based sense of their own world. By middle and high school grade levels, a student's ability to be self-directed relies solely in the coaching of basic and intermediate concepts of self, social, and societal expectations as they increase in their ability to reason hypothetically and understand more complex systems that support their own mastery of skills and ownership of learning.

An example from my own classroom in the upper elementary grade levels is one that involves my students who are independently using resources but are unable to tell me how they are using those resources. I've found that this is a common example for all grade levels and a clear sign that these students are still in need of coaching and not yet able to be completely self-directed. These students may have shown their mastery of a different resource for a task that targets a specific skill or standard and are attempting to apply that same learning to a different resource, task, or skill. Unfortunately, they are unsure exactly how that resource is to be used for what task and for what skill or standard. This is where I would coach the student to work through the first two areas of Self-Directed Learning to identify the skill or standard, exactly what task is targeting that skill or standard, and how the resource is being used to help the student learn. It is in these situations that the difference between *playing* and *learning* may need to be distinguished through the context of various situations.

For me as a teacher, recognizing the difference between playing and discovering with classroom resources takes patience, leniency, and, most important, a classroom culture that develops supportive communication skills to help students keep each other in check. Different teachers may consider different ways to teach these communication skills in order to specifically address language and contexts appropriate for their students. However, the objective measures that serve as a foundation for these communication skills can be found in stages of social and emotional learning and cognitive development. Students in early elementary grade levels will be taught skills differently than students in upper elementary; the same goes for middle and high school grade levels.

Another aspect of resources from a whole-class perspective is the consideration of value toward Self-Directed Learning as a learning environment. Specifically, I focus on the difference between a tool and a toy, how any object or resource can be treated as a toy, and the resulting consequences *on the learning environment* as opposed to the individual when classroom resources are mistreated. Students who understand the value in a self-directed learning environment have a more intrinsic means of motivation for ensuring other students are not misusing resources. The motivation here becomes not one of individual punishment by the command of the teacher but as one of whole class self-redirection by keeping each other accountable for the sake of a desired learning environment.

The way I avoid having to shift backward from a Self-Directed Learning classroom environment is to teach all students how to identify off-task behaviors and how to kindly redirect their peers when they notice it happening. I am not providing here a specific list of behaviors and strategies because every classroom in any school, district, region, or state will have different cultural and social considerations. As I follow the academic standards, and address social-emotional components, while also addressing the human development of my students, I am able to utilize situational awareness in order to support the emotions, coping strategies, and development of my students' sense of self-efficacy, self-reflection, and goal-setting. This eventually builds a customized peer-based support system of accountability. I must admit that a lot of my time is spent guiding my students outside of academic instruction, but I find that this builds ownership in student learning that has long-term effects on both student learning and positive classroom culture. This approach is embedded in the next chapter on behavioral coaching.

STRATEGIES

I often get questions on the difference between Making a Plan and Strategies. When it comes to developing strategies, the distinction is between the specific task as part of a plan that targets a standard or skill and the strategy used to support the learning of that standards-based task.

One example involves third-grade rounding. It is the first time that rounding is introduced to students (according to the Common Core State Standard – 3.NBT.1). A possible task to track growth of learning could be as simple as a Q&A challenge between peers where students would write a two-digit number for the other student to round. The student may use resources that include pencils and paper and base ten blocks, but it is the *strategy* that will help them use those resources to participate in the task and develop mastery of the standard. A potential strategy might involve drawing a number line with a *tens* or *hundreds* number on either end that are closest to the number being rounded. Another strategy involves changing that number line into a *mountain* that highlights the middle of that number line to assist the student in visualizing which way a number is to be rounded. A third example might involve a rounding poem to help students track a procedure for rounding.

With each strategy that is taught for each standard or skill, the key component with regard to self-directed learning is tracking which strategies target which standards. This begins with my own mastery of the standards and knowing in advance which tasks are best suited for each standard. This then allows me to identify which resources are necessary and prepare effective strategies for mastering the standards.

As I teach a grade level for the first time, I track which strategies work well with my students. I create a chart that shows each standard and what tasks, resources, and strategies are associated with that standard. There is often overlap between these breakdowns, but it helps to clarify for me as much as it helps my students to identify what has resulted in student learning such that students can refer to those strategies and resources to create for themselves the kind of self-directed learning environment that works for them.

STANDARD	TASK(S)	RESOURCE(S)	STRATEGIES
3.NBT.1 Rounding	Q&A Challenge	Pencil/Paper; Base Ten Blocks	Rounding Poem; "Mountain" Number Line

The students in my classrooms are not required to track strategies for each standard and are not reprimanded in any way for not tracking strategies. However, throughout the year, I consistently guide students in reflecting on which strategies are best suited for each standard. What I find is that most students develop an inherent desire to show independence and pride in learning. The difficulty here is in identifying when this independence is causing students to struggle in identifying strategies that are best suited in assisting students as they practice a skill.

This idea of identifying strategies and associating them to specific resources and tasks inherently develops a critical component in developing self-directed learners. Because teachers, schools, and districts approach instruction in different ways, with different curricula, and various supplemental materials and resources, it is virtually impossible to address and incorporate one set of standards-based strategies specific to all classrooms across the country. It is the exercise in identifying strategies and expecting students to communicate which strategies they are choosing to use to benefit their own mastery of specific standards that is the critical component for this area of Self-Directed Learning.

PRODUCT

This final area of Self-Directed Learning addresses assessment practices. Once the standards and skills are addressed, tasks and progress tracked, resources responsibly utilized, and strategies intentionally practiced, having students show mastery of standards is an exclusive area of Self-Directed Learning that may look different than traditional assessment practices. The main difference in a self-directed learning environment involves students and the freedom provided in showing mastery through a product specific to their strengths, then followed by adapting student mastery to more traditional written and oral testing environments. This main difference directly translates to a standards-based philosophy and approach toward formative and summative assessment practices.

When teachers begin to shift from traditional to self-directed formative assessments, it is important to work toward balancing freedom and accountability when it comes to individual student mastery of each skill or standard. Students are not directly instructed to create self-directed products of mastery without showing at least a developing sense of all other aspects. To be clear, students are not given a list of possible products for illustrating mastery of all the various skills and standards and expected to *figure it out*. As students internalize the various academic and social-emotional skills, they will likely discover, or be introduced to, various means of producing works of skill mastery relevant to the skill or idea being practiced. The more students learn to expound on possible products of mastery with each passing year, the more students can share with each other and build on the mastery of products they experience (either themselves or through their peers). As students prove to themselves, to their peers, and to a lesser extent to their teachers their mastery of various skills and track their growth toward proficiency, it will be important that students also recognize the need for *synthesizing*, or adapting, that mastery to meet more traditional assessment formats. This is not to deny students the value of their growth but to offer students a means for identifying how learning can be mastered in various ways, including that of more traditional formats. The approach for balancing such a variety of assessment opportunities will look different for different teachers. The idea is to develop in students the intrinsic desire for wanting to learn by creating products that show their mastery of ideas and skills.

It is important to keep in mind the goal, or vision, of Self-Directed Learning. The goal, or vision, is for students to enter the classroom and first know exactly what they are expected to learn, how what they're learning connects to prior years, and how that is preparing them for what's to come. Self-directed students can then utilize strategies that promote interdependent collaboration among peers in order to identify and track goals, consider available and appropriate resources as tools for learning, communicate specific strategies for concepts, and produce relevant evidence that validates the readiness for standards-based assessments.

CHAPTER 5 (PART 1)

Behavioral Coaching

When Social and Emotional Learning overlaps with Cognitive and Psychosocial Development, they create a Secondary Concept: Behavioral Coaching and Intervention. This concept addresses those students whose behaviors fall outside of a classroom's general behavior expectations.

This concept is one with which I apply a particular philosophy: fear only serves to suppress negative student behavior while positive student behavior is promoted through coaching and intervention. This philosophy does not dismiss punitive measures for misbehavior—it only serves to include coaching and intervention to meet the social-emotional development of my students. Another philosophy that I apply is one that examines the conformity of student behavior and the effect of positive and negative reinforcement toward students whose behavior may *not* be considered disruptive.

It is important to note that general behavior expectations are relative to a teacher's classroom expectations within a school's framework of values and that this section does not promote a specific set of general behavior expectations.

It is also important to know that this philosophy is by no means *new*—similar philosophy has been shared for quite some time. For example, in the book *The Manual of Child Development* (1955), it is stated that it "is not true that any sort of punishment that suddenly occurs to you will do. To have any constructive value, a punishment must follow certain principles" (p. 421). This is only to highlight the idea that *off the cuff* management of humans has never sufficed and will never suffice.

CHANGING ROLE OF THE CLASSROOM TEACHER

In the following paragraphs, I will be highlighting my first years of teaching and the struggles in developing my own sense of general behavior expectations. The point of these paragraphs is to illustrate the idea that a classroom can be guided in developing a relative equilibrium of student and teacher expectations. It is this idea of general behavior expectations that will serve as the basis for my ideas on behavioral coaching and intervention.

In my experience, there has always been a percentage of students who have challenged my classroom learning environment through various degrees of misbehaviors. The number of my instructional minutes that have been hijacked due to outbursts, inappropriate interactions, or reactions, has caused seemingly endless amounts of disruption in past classrooms. In short, a small percentage of students seem to have caused the highest percentage of decreased learning time in my classroom, on average, over time.

The question I ask myself is this: how can each of these humans, regardless of age, have had that much power over a room full of other humans? There is no single answer because every one of these individual humans had strengths and qualities that sparked interest and regard from their peers. Sometimes these students were genuinely funny or charming and sometimes they were utterly obnoxious and routinely disruptive. What is important in that last sentence is that the other students sometimes had opposite experiences—a disruptive behavior that I found utterly obnoxious and routinely disruptive may have come across to students as genuinely funny or charming.

Self-Reflection of Past Experience

During my earliest years of teaching, I recall punishing students for their disruptive behavior in accordance with my school's framework of values and flowchart for behavior management. I would address the individual student who was *misbehaving* with no regard to the sensationalism that was being instilled in other students. In my frustration, I would declare further punishments for *any* student who felt such disruptions were funny or charming.

What I failed to consider in those early years of teaching was that a disruption was not a personal attack on me but rather a form of communication that the content served little purpose for that student. In addressing this student, I provided the rest of the students a distraction that *they were unable to challenge* because I was deemed the authority in the classroom and the students were not in a position to correct my reactions to a disruption.

In my own self-reflection, I considered different approaches to disruptions beyond that of a simple reminder followed by a series of punishments. I began experimenting with halting a lesson completely, having the class put away all materials, and discuss with them their thoughts on whether the lesson or activity had any value to them, whether there was any value to the content, and whether what they have learned previously connects to what they are learning today.

The general consensus over so many of these class discussions can be summarized into two statements:

1. Students know that a teacher's structured lessons will come and go like clockwork.

2. Students know that their own learning is ultimately up to them to do the reading, complete the practice, have the discussions, and explain the material.

To my students, what they did during my lessons was really a matter of keeping quiet long enough until they can go back to doing whatever they were going to do anyway, whether it was focusing on the lesson's reading and practicing whatever skill they felt they need to practice, or perhaps a task completely unrelated to school.

The disruptions and misbehaviors that occurred in my classroom had little to do with my training as a teacher (e.g., engagement, instruction, small groups, exit tickets). It wasn't anything specific about me personally nor was it any individual part of my lesson planning and use of a particular instructional model. What I discovered was that the disruptions and misbehaviors had more to do with impatience and disrespect toward *the approach to teaching and learning* that was being communicated through my actions.

> There was a dual disconnect between what I was doing and what I expected students to do while also between what students were doing and what students expected me to do.

As I look at my classrooms of more recent years and as I continue to adapt standards-based and social-emotional practices to develop a self-directed learning environment, it has been most interesting to note how student disruptions and misbehaviors have not been eliminated. Instead, what has changed is an increase in student self-efficacy, ownership of learning, and support for their peers; what has improved is my perspective toward my role as a classroom teacher—shifting from distributing punishment for misbehavior to coaching guidance through experiences. What I've come to realize is that my role is not a teacher of academics but a student coach that teaches my team of students how to win each day by working together to achieve the goals that improve their own learning of skills that will become increasingly difficult with each passing year.

GENERAL BEHAVIOR EXPECTATIONS

This idea of behavioral coaching has become the foundation for my direct academic instruction. Yes, I do occasionally teach skills from the front of the classroom to all students; I do teach small groups and individuals as well as allow students to work independently on separate standards as needed. The benefits of behavioral coaching in the classroom does not replace instructional models as much as it provides a philosophy for approaching the development of an intended set of general behavior expectations. General behavior expectations are not Rules and Consequences. These are the day-to-day behaviors one might expect from those involved in a learning environment—students, teachers, parents, etc. The behaviors we might expect in a kindergarten classroom may have some similarities to what may be expected in a middle or high school classroom. Some schools may promote general statements regarding safety and responsibility while others may provide lists of specific behaviors—for example, how students and teachers are to simply enter a classroom. As I reference general behavior expectations, it is important to remember that, generally speaking, we do expect all other humans to behave in certain ways in order for us to feel safe, to maintain friendships, and support not only our own goals but the goals of others for the benefit of the larger community.

The biggest takeaway as I explore the general behavior expectations that exist in my classroom is that my primary role as a teacher is building a sense of community by which all students develop value and ownership of their learning. My general expectations for behavior have less to do with how academics are developed and more to do with how students develop socially and emotionally so that academics can then be approached with purpose and intent. It now seems like every day I am tasked with finding ways to adjust my approach toward developing in my students the awareness and management skills to support each other to stay on track, recognize effects of their own reactions to each other, and empower each other to create a learning environment of academic reciprocity that benefits all students in the form of academic success.

At the start of a school year, teachers know the struggle of developing classroom procedures. It is equally challenging for the students to become comfortable with a particular classroom's procedures. As teachers, we design procedures to help maintain order in the classroom and recognize that the majority of students have a basic understanding that rules are to be followed to avoid punishment. As stated on the previous page, because teachers are deemed an authority figure in the classroom, the majority of students are generally unwilling to challenge a teacher's decisions or comment on their behaviors.

As teachers, we consider our classroom's general behavior expectations as reasonable. It is reasonable to assert procedures for sharpening a pencil in order to minimize a student's ability to disrupt even a minute of learning. It is reasonable to declare a series of required procedures (e.g., hands to yourself, arms to the side, light footsteps, lips zipped, stay in one line) for having a class of twenty or thirty students walk down a hallway where classes are in session. It is reasonable to designate specific gestures for student requests to minimize disruption (bathroom, water, etc.), expect students to enter a classroom quietly and attentively, and have students in assigned seats so the teacher can quickly scan the room to take attendance.

General behavior expectations, for the majority of students, are not a problem and are understood by students to simply be rules they must follow—*because school*. However, we teachers must acknowledge that, because these behavior expectations can be extremely specific to the contexts that they are assigned, they may be directly opposed to students' inherent desire for social interaction and amusement. *Remain silent while lined up in the hallway outside of classrooms in session* is a very specific expectation in a specific context. Consider whether those students also line up outside perhaps after recess but are allowed to talk to each other in line because it is not in the hallway and away from classrooms in session. This might cause some degree of cognitive dissonance for a number of students who forget in which particular context of standing in line they are expected to remain silent.

There are so many general behavior expectations that this one example of *remaining silent in line* does not begin to address the vast array of student considerations with regard to student disruptions in response to the specific general behavior expectations of a particular classroom. The intention here is that, for the majority of students, general behavior expectations will not be so demanding that students are unable to abide by them, if not simply to avoid reprimand. However, there will likely be a percentage of students who may not find particular behavior expectations reasonable, and it is important to note that this percentage may overlap with a small number of that majority that are abiding by rules reluctantly.

When it comes to general behavior expectations, there will be a number of students who either take an extraordinarily long time to accept and abide by these expectations or assert their disapproval through either words or actions. It is for these students that a fear-based series of reprimands and punishments prove ineffective. For this reason, the concept of behavioral coaching (in-class) and intervention (classroom and school-wide) may provide the positive communication of behavior expectations that will help these students conform to the general behavior expectations of a school or classroom.

BEHAVIORAL COACHING [IN-CLASS APPROACH]

This approach to behavioral coaching is not unlike other programs and products that promote positive behavior intervention and support. The purpose of this approach is to promote value and understanding of a desired classroom learning environment. This means that all of the general behavior expectations that exist and are effective for the majority of students but seemingly ineffective for a small percentage of students must be part of a larger philosophy that is able to be communicated at the level of language appropriate for these students.

Coaching Starts With the Coach

Our actions as humans cause reactions in our environment that can become obstacles if they keep us from achieving our desired goals. These obstacles can be external forces (e.g., objects, tasks, personalities) as well as internal forces (e.g., self-doubt, trust, perseverance). Obstacles are both the cause of, and a result of, life experience. We, as adults, know these obstacles can be overcome because we have experienced them, seen our way through them, and came out on the other side with either a positive or negative perspective of the struggle we experienced.

What I have come to recognize is that understanding the means by which I have overcome obstacles, through recognizing the depth, complexity, and patience required, better prepares me to overcome more challenging obstacles in my own life while simultaneously coaching my students on how they can overcome their obstacles. In order to do this, I must know my own self as well as I know my academic content so that I may coach my students to strengthen their own mastery toward becoming a Self-Directed Learner.

This section serves as an overview of how my own ongoing efforts to master social-emotional components in myself relates to my ability to implement behavioral coaching in my classroom.

It is important to recognize that, just like academics, telling students how to solve a problem is less helpful than guiding them toward solving a problem themselves. I have, in the past, been assigned a grade level that I had not previously taught. This required preparation of academic content, strategies, resources, project planning, among many other things, and there were still aspects of that grade level that I had to learn through experience and work with students to adjust and meet their academic needs. When it comes to behavioral coaching, much the same can be expected with regard to preparing for a school year of new obstacles and helping students learn to overcome them. My own awareness and management of self, social, and societal social-emotional components is the first step in preparing for behavior coaching. The following paragraphs list suggestions for teachers to consider developing SEL components in themselves.

Identify and Manage Emotions

Determine for yourself what words most accurately describe your feelings throughout the day. This may seem superfluous to some teachers as they may believe feelings have little to do with the academic topics they are instructing. However, not only may this improve the already positive relationships you have with some students, it will help to strengthen the relationship you have with so many more students who enter your classroom expecting to learn how to be a student in your classroom.

Develop coping strategies that work for you in the contexts you most need them. Teaching can be stressful—and so can learning! Being open about the use of coping strategies for overwhelming emotions may seem to some teachers as a sign of weakness, but keep in mind that students are not the antagonists of a classroom's story. It may be enough for some teachers to simply identify the emotion and appropriate coping strategy in reaction to a student experiencing an overwhelming emotion in reaction to something related or unrelated to the academic expectations on a given day.

Self-Efficacy and Improvement

Incorporate your strengths and interests into your classroom learning environment. Your classroom may be heavily academic in its decoration and arrangement. Providing even a minor insight into an aspect of your life in which you find pride and satisfaction beyond academic topics can improve the ability of students to find joy not only in being in your classroom but also in reaching out to you as their teacher.

Be open about your own ongoing attempts to receive training and assistance in learning new things. We want our students to be open to asking for help but sometimes feel that asking for help communicates to others that they are less than perfect. Your ability to communicate your own need to seek help with things provides context for your students to attempt similar approaches to improvement.

Self-Reflection and Goal-Setting

Be transparent in your goals for the classroom and be open in your reflection as to how you are adjusting those goals throughout the year. This idea of setting goals is inherent as our role as classroom teachers. There are typically specific academic goals for the school year that may be organized into trimester or quarter expectations. Presenting a means for students to identify where we are as teachers in reaching our goals for classroom success may help our students in adjusting their goals for what they must do for their own success in the classroom.

Empathy and Perspective

Be an active listener to your students concerns. A teacher's ability to empathize with every student becomes difficult for those teachers that have up to (or over) a hundred students walk through their doors each day. However, this component is not about giving in to every student's emotional need. Rather, recognizing in some students a lack of empathy can be enough to inquire about what is going on in that student's life that is causing this development. Perhaps one or two students in a couple different classes are showing signs of distress for various reasons that seem to be affecting their schoolwork. Being able to approach these students ready to listen will not require unnecessary leniency in academic expectations but perhaps pairing these students in specific classroom groups may provide the positive support enough to help these students get through a difficult time. The perspective by which you approach a student empathetically may be enough for some students to feel that the classroom is not an unsafe place to be.

Interpersonal Skills

Be the kind of adult you want your students to become. Imagine your students walking around with furrowed eyebrows, avoiding eye contact with other people, and quickly going from classroom to classroom completely focused on their work. This may be the polar opposite of some students you observe that walk around bright-eyed, stopping to talk to everybody, and meandering from class to class not sure what assignments are due when or where. The fact is that your students will never become you—they will become *them*! Yet, the kind of them will be influenced by every interaction and relationship they have throughout their life. Ignoring your students will not exclude you from the impact you may have on them just as being the most interesting and entertaining teacher may not impact all of your students to also become the most interesting and entertaining people in the world. All we can do is provide the motivation to believe that positivity and hard work in the face of conflict and challenge can result in positive relationships and success from day to day as we strive for larger goals.

Conflict Resolution

Be willing to recognize and refer conflicts appropriately. It is unreasonable for a teacher to solve all of their students' problems. As students become older and more susceptible to more complex (and more subtle) conflicts, students will also become more capable of approaching conflicts with specific resolution strategies. As the classroom teacher, we may consider ourselves the king or queen of our domain and attempt to solve all of our student issues ourselves. Our ability to talk through strategies for conflict and resolution can help with small conflicts within the classroom in ways that may diffuse the conflict and keep it from becoming a large conflict. Our ability to recognize conflict and follow up on potential escalation is as important as our ability to help students learn to recognize such things. It is also important that we as teachers recognize that conflicts may require administrator intervention as they may have insight across the campus and into other classrooms that may serve to resolve the conflict much more efficiently. That said, it is important that we understand what kinds of conflicts may exist and what resolution strategies are appropriate so that we can distinguish degrees of conflict and communicate with our colleagues and administration about what might be going on with our students.

Responsibility (Rules and Consequences)

Be able to connect with the "real world." The control over behaviors that we expect students to exercise can sometimes seem circumstantial, like these behaviors only make sense on a school campus. However, we must keep in mind that standing in line is not strictly a school rule—adults out in the world are standing in line all the time! Although adults don't raise their hand before they ask somebody a question, we certainly don't shout across a bank to get a teller's attention. When we see an item that isn't ours sitting on the ground out on the playground, we either take it to the lost and found or leave it there so the owner of that item can go back and get it. The same goes for an item we see on the ground outside of a business—we'll either take it in to that business to see if somebody dropped it or leave it there in hopes that the owner of the item retraces their steps. All of this is to instill the idea that what we want this world to become is mirrored on school campuses. The risks that students take while in school are exercising these boundaries of societal responsibility. Likewise, the way in which we as teachers respond to students might be taken as society's response to their civil and uncivil actions. Being able to communicate that so that it is appropriate for the age or grade level of the student is important for us as teachers to remember.

Caring and Citizenship (Community Building)

Be an advocate for the community in which you teach. We can't wait for students to be emotionally well-balanced and empathetically capable before we concern them with what it means to help their community. The mindset of recognizing that we rely on the help and support of our community leaders takes time and experience. It is important for students to recognize the role of citizens within their own communities and the assistance citizens provide for their own community through resources and services. Defining a community by the citizens that make up that community is a difficult concept to learn from a book. Providing opportunities for students to benefit from each other can start with teaching students the value of assisting others and doing the work around the school that makes the school what we want it to become.

Beliefs and Behaviors

Note: The ideas presented in this particular section may be rooted in concepts such as Behavioral Decision Theory and confirmation bias but are not intended to provide instruction in any specific theory. The intention of this particular section is to provide insight into how behavioral coaching may account for the difference between beliefs and behaviors for students in our classrooms.

Any student action is a behavior. To train specific student behaviors, teachers typically develop a series of punishments and rewards. When a student behavior takes place, part of our job as teachers is to determine whether that behavior is appropriate or not and respond accordingly with either a punishment or reward until the expected behavior becomes habit.

Decisions of students in lower elementary grade levels may be more susceptible to emotional persuasion since their prefrontal cortex responsible for logical decision making has only recently started to develop and won't fully mature until their mid-20's. This is not meant to imply that lower elementary students are unable to control their behaviors; the approach for developing the beliefs and behaviors in lower elementary students may look different for students in the upper elementary grade levels and above.

Consider this statement: *A belief is an acceptance that a statement is true.*

If you are to believe that this statement is true, you may consider this a belief.

Consider this statement: *It is inappropriate for a student taking a test to talk to another student during that test.*

If you are to believe that this statement is false in any way, you may not consider this a belief. If this statement depends on even a single variable, then it is likely that you believe that this statement is false.

As students become more capable of challenging rules logically and concretely (read more about Piaget's *Concrete Operational Stage*, pg. 52), they will likely begin to challenge the very rules they claim to believe they follow. It is this development of assertively challenging belief in rules, as statements, in the upper elementary school years that becomes a critical period of time for behaviors and beliefs. Keep in mind that students are working through a psychosocial stage of *industry vs inferiority* and will be susceptible to bouts of both overconfidence and self-deprecation. For this reason, punishments for a rule in which a student does not believe can cause confusion and distrust in those assigning punishment. The popular student phrase, *the teacher got me in trouble* is common for this reason. The student made a decision that was based on a belief that contradicted what the school believes without exception.

So how can a teacher get at the beliefs that student decisions seem to be based on in order to have an effect on student patterns of behavior? The following image introduces the connection between extrinsic and intrinsic motivation and the relation to beliefs, decisions, and behaviors.

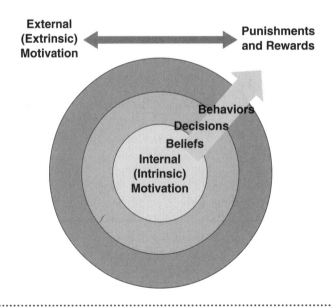

This image highlights three main factors: beliefs, decisions, and behaviors; this image also places these factors in the context of their relationship to intrinsic versus extrinsic motivation. The intended purpose of punishments and rewards is to adjust behavior. However, adjusting behavior via extrinsic motivation alone may have little effect on decision making and little to no effect on beliefs. Punishments are generally fear-based external motivators intended to persuade a person to *not* do something or to *stop* a person from doing something. Rewards are generally intended to be joy-based external motivators meant to persuade a person to start, continue, and complete various tasks. Neither are best suited for accessing internal (intrinsic) motivation for our students, especially with regard to academic, emotional, and social expectations set for them.

What the preceding image hopes to illustrate in relation to this chapter is that whether a child adjusts their behaviors according to external rewards and punishments does not guarantee that those students are adjusting their beliefs toward those behaviors. This means that students are likely associating the idea of following rules to the person(s) issuing the rewards and punishments resulting from following rules and may not automatically apply the same behaviors to other situations if the same rewards and punishments are not in place. This becomes readily apparent when a substitute teacher enters a classroom. Students often feel the general behavior expectations no longer need to be exercised because the typical rewards or punishments enforced by their teacher are no longer present. Their beliefs, their internal motivators toward the general behavior expectations, have not been changed—only their behaviors are adjusted and only based on specific external motivators.

The question here is not whether punishments or rewards are effective motivators. The question here is why, for some students, punishments and rewards do not seem to have their intended effects on student perspectives toward meeting the general behavior expectations set by a school or classroom teacher.

While behavioral coaching will benefit nearly all students, the students for whom behavioral coaching will have the most benefit are those whose beliefs fall farthest outside of the general behavior expectations. These students do not believe the expectations are truths that they must value—they disagree with the general behavior expectations, and therefore are most likely to feel disenfranchised by a school's system of rewards and punishments.

In order to help these students to recognize the value of these behaviors, they may need more than a list of punishments and rewards associated with a school's general behavior expectations. They may also need to discuss—consistently and often—the reasoning for the existence and benefits of these expectations. Such discussions will likely require multiple sessions both in class and perhaps in an intervention setting. Please also keep in mind that concepts of empathy and perspective, interpersonal skills, and societal responsibility and community play a role in shaping such beliefs and that students weak in such areas of social-emotional components may struggle the most with any efforts to access their beliefs and change their behaviors.

For example, take the reasonable expectation of not talking while lined up outside of classrooms. If one of these few students repeatedly talks in line in the hallways while classes are in session, they may not believe that their talking is enough of a distraction to those classes for them to stop having the conversations they want to have. Telling the student that their talking in line is unacceptable, or wrong, may result in questions or confrontations. Telling the student that their talking in line is disruptive to other classes in session may result in the student explaining how one outside voice is not enough to completely disrupt an entire class. Such conversations with the student serve as not only a vehicle for other students to now consider such logical exceptions but is now only shifting the student's conversation with the other student to a conversation with you in the hallway instead!

As students get older, such minor challenges to general behavior expectations will begin to transfer these beliefs toward more nuanced exceptions to simple rules—especially if the beliefs in the value of these rules are not developed.

The hard part is acknowledging that these students are already cognitively aware of the expectations and that it is the emotional side of believing in the value of these expectations that must be addressed. In order to target this emotional part of a belief, the student may need to not only experience the value of these expectations but consider the value of these expectations from the perspective of their peers.

Reasoning of facts and consideration of others may not be enough to change the value of a person's beliefs—even in a student. In the podcast Hidden Brain, episode 64 "I'm Right, You're Wrong" (March 13, 2017) highlights Tali Sharot, a cognitive neuroscientist at University College London. In this episode, Sharot is introduced as having spent "years studying the way we process information and why we often reach biased conclusions. She says it's surprisingly difficult for us to change one another's minds, no matter how much data we present. But just a little bit of emotion, that can go a long way." Sharot describes the idea of confirmation bias as "our tendency to take in any kind of data that confirms our prior convictions and to disregard data that does not conform to what we already believe." She continues by saying that there are "four factors that determine whether we're going to change our beliefs—our old belief, our confidence in that old belief, the new piece of data and our confidence in that piece of data."

Teachers can use this perspective to help get at the beliefs our students hold about the general behavior expectations we have set across a school campus. We may be able to gauge the level of confidence our students already hold in their current belief toward general expected behaviors by having class discussions where students explain their perspective in several different contexts. Again, for lower elementary students, their emotional reactions to behavior expectations are likely to be best received with emotional persuasion. This gauge in student beliefs is better served for older students who are learning how to logically discredit the value of general behavior expectations.

If the beliefs of our students are strong enough to withstand thought exercises in various contexts, perhaps it is worth considering an adjustment to a general behavior expectation that accounts for their rationale. However, if the beliefs of our students are unable to withstand the majority of contexts for such thought exercises, the few contexts by which their beliefs are held can then be looked at as exceptions that may or may not apply to the context of our school environment.

The value in going to such lengths as to dissect beliefs and values of what we as teachers might see as generally accepted expectations for student behaviors is to provide a forum by which students can be given the language and structure for making such arguments themselves. As we revisit these conversations throughout the year and give students the opportunity to practice speaking about these issues, the majority of students who already shared beliefs in the general behavior expectations may begin speaking out against those students who repeatedly forget or disregard those expectations.

Coaching Student Behaviors

In my classroom, behavioral coaching can happen at all times of the school day. Every behavior, positive and negative, is an opportunity for all students to be coached—all at once, in small groups, or individually. It is up to teachers to determine the depth and frequency of coaching in classrooms depending on the needs of students. For me, I spend most of my first couple of weeks on behavioral coaching rather than academic instruction. Because the first month is generally accepted as a time to focus on rules and procedures, I find that increased behavioral coaching the first trimester causes the second and third trimester to be extremely productive. Academically, this tends to have little impact on the progress of students due to the standards-based grading approach to identifying and tracking student progress. When I also consider the roll out of the self-directed learning environment, the first few months are typically spent on developing the beliefs students will need to internalize in order to be successful as a self-directed learner.

When coaching in-class, especially at the beginning of the year, whenever a student interacts with you or anybody around them, that is an opportunity for coaching—at any grade level. For example, a student who gets up and goes to the bathroom without raising their hand but not disrupting the classroom may result in other students watching this happen and considering the implications. Younger students may *tattle* if they have had other teachers require permission. Older students may simply apply that as a precedent for a classroom policy that they will likely apply at a later time (perhaps with variations to further test the boundaries). That student's action of getting up and going to the bathroom without permission is an opportunity to stop academic instruction, discuss not only my actual policy on that behavior but clarify questions regarding the value of this policy and allows me to connect with my students on a level deeper and more meaningful than one of a basic authority figure. In my experience, the beginning weeks often have students not entirely comfortable in the new classroom setting which means they are fairly quiet and attentive those first few weeks. This is all the more beneficial for the teacher to clarify with reasoning and hypotheticals that can guide the class through the rationale for classroom policies intended to improve student learning. Any policy that can be outed as an unreasonable policy by a student is likely to be exactly the kind of policy that may need adjusting— this also serves to build trust between students and their teacher as partners (although unequal in authority) of a meaningful learning environment.

Examples of behaviors that call for behavioral coaching may include: intentional burping, calling answers out of turn, misuse of resources, various negative words/actions toward others—anything the disrupts student learning. Whatever the case may be, it is important that I prepare to recognize the self- or social-awareness and skills being challenged, the effect it is having on overall student learning, and my ability to critically talk the student through why that student is allowing such behaviors to continue. Eventually, this must go beyond behaviors of individual students and include behaviors of conformity that are equally damaging to the learning environment.

Examples of behaviors that teachers may want to teach to students throughout the school year may include (though not limited to):

1. quietly and politely informing a peer that it is not the time to [student misbehavior];

2. offer peers academic support during independent class time or outside of class;

3. look the student in the eyes and ask the student what is wrong and be prepared to listen if they want to tell you;

4. be prepared to discuss with the teacher without fear of punishment any problems that may need to be addressed in the classroom for the sake of all learners.

These actions can be difficult to instill in students as they require beliefs that these actions have value. It is especially difficult when middle or high school students with little experience in these types of peer-based support systems are taught this way for the first time. I find that the upper elementary students (following a strong K–2 foundation) is an excellent opportunity to develop peer-based support systems in the classroom given their cognitive and psychosocial development at those age ranges. As these students get older, if these systems are not developed, it will be a struggle to make this process attractive as they may develop social anxiety over ideas of *tattling* or *snitching* (as opposed to the value of wanting to help a friend or classmate succeed). While it may take longer for older students to appropriate these actions in their classrooms, the introduction of these ideas into your classroom learning environment can potentially instill these ideas in an increasing number of students over time.

This brings me to another good point: the debunking of student-created myths and misappropriated slang. Too often, students hear certain words and phrases from peers or older siblings that they do not understand and use them incorrectly to define situations or people. These words and phrases must be explained and put into context to avoid students misappropriating these words and complicating what would otherwise be a minor altercation. For example, I often must clarify the word *snitch* as it seems to have passed the test of time and is still being misused the same as it has been for several decades. For students who claim they do not want to tell on other students for fear of being called this word, I calmly instruct them on the subtle difference between being a snitch—and being a friend. While my explanation includes a sketch and several illustrated examples, the basic gist is this:

> A snitch may run away from a situation to tell on a student with or without the intention of getting them in trouble while a friend may run away from a situation with the sole intent of getting their friend help from a trusted authority figure. The basic takeaway is the difference between a friend that keeps a look out while you do something that isn't good for others, and a friend that redirects you toward actions that are more productive and fun for everybody involved.

This explanation does not omit the existence of such friends or slang terms but rather puts them in context such that students can determine what kind of students they want to be (and what kind of students they want to have) in their classroom and learn to show this want through their actions and reactions.

This level of awareness and ownership serves to develop allies in your students, generally those students who want to learn but are not equipped with the social skills to defend their right to learn. As more students become empowered to stand up for this right, it spurs other students who may have been on the fence to join the cause and create a learning environment that makes them proud to be in school because it has become a place they have created through their own intent and purpose.

CHAPTER 5 (PART 2)

Behavioral Inclusion and Intervention

BEHAVIORAL INCLUSION

I typically have discussions with colleagues about *academic* inclusion that includes all students in a fully inclusive academic instructional model. Here, I would like to introduce a model for *behavioral* inclusion that, in some ways, may mirror that of the academic inclusion model though primarily focuses on the social-emotional development of all students in a general education classroom environment.

There are five student tiers in my inclusive model that addresses both academic and behavioral inclusion: TAGs—Talented and Gifted Students; GenEds—General Education Students; RTIIs—Response to Instruction and Intervention Students; ELLs—English Language Learner Students; and SpEds—Special Education Students.

General behavior expectations (discussed in Chapter 5, Part 1 as well as later in this chapter) extend across all five student tiers. Each tier then extends the general behavior expectations to allow for individual strengths or needs that will shape the overall classroom learning environment for all students. This is initially a difficult concept—implementing strategies that support individual needs for all students including those who may not seem to need them. As we look at examples, it will show how threading strategies that target individual needs into the general classroom learning environment not only makes it easier to include those individual students in classroom learning but also makes concept-strengthening strategies and approaches publicly available to all students without stigma or reproach. This idea of behavioral inclusion offers an organization for behavioral inclusion that can be adapted with thoughtful intent to fit any preferred organization of tiers within a classroom or a school.

As a teacher, it is important to adapt my general behavior expectations to include these student tiers—it is this that makes behavioral inclusion so important. By being malleable and transparent in my general behavior expectations, I can help all of my students develop an inclusive learning environment that meets the needs of all students. It is this aspect of student ownership of not only academic inclusion but of behavioral inclusion that lends itself to creating a self-directed learning environment.

It must also be made aware that a behavioral inclusion model praises understanding, not conformity. There may be a percentage of students in my classroom (across all tiers) that conform to my general behavior expectations without reflection or growth. Keeping quiet and completing worksheets may provide a quiet and productive learning environment, but it becomes difficult for those students to exercise social interaction and academic reciprocation, key components to a self-directed classroom. It is important to also identify such conformity in students as it may potentially result in missed academic or social-emotional growth opportunities.

Range of General Behavior Expectations

Structuring general behavior expectations for a behavioral inclusive environment is not as overwhelming as it may initially seem. Recognize that grade-level classrooms will have a particular range of behaviors related to student cognitive and psychosocial development. As discussed in Chapter 3, lower elementary and middle school grade levels may see a larger percentage of students developing through overlapping cognitive and psychosocial stages while upper elementary and high school grade levels may see a larger percentage of students developing through single stages. As classroom teachers, the range or capacity for our general behavior expectations will find its limits in our perspective toward the development occurring in the students assigned to our classrooms.

For example, as a kindergarten teacher, you may need only to consider what your five-year-old students can generally be expected to do. To what depth can your five-year-old students analyze a story that is read to them? How many consecutive directions can your five-year-old students follow at the start of the year versus the end of the year? How quickly can your five-year-old students recover when feeling overwhelmed by a task they find exceptionally challenging? You will likely be able to create a range of general behavior expectations based on such considerations that support a behavioral inclusive learning environment specific to your five-year-old students.

An eleventh-grade class may need only consider what a sixteen-year-old can generally be expected to do. To what depth can your sixteen-year-olds analyze a story that they have chosen to read? How many consecutive directions can a sixteen-year-old follow to achieve preset goals for the week, month, or semester? How quickly can a sixteen-year-old recoup when challenged with academic and personal tasks that they may find exceptionally challenging?

Teachers, again, will likely be able to give a range of student capacity based on any number of variables.

It does not make sense to use a student's assigned grade level to label a person's cognitive or behavioral capacity as simply *below* or *above* strict grade-level expectations. This is because grade levels are age-based, and students are not preprogrammed to develop the same emotional and social skills according to the number of revolutions Earth makes around the sun. It is more important to monitor growth over time according to the development of individual skills rather than age-based grade-level assignments. Self-management and social relationships, for example, are fluid development to be monitored for growth more than grade-level proficiency. Recognizing ranges for expectations of behavior allows for patience and understanding to be modeled by both teachers and students.

Observing General Behavioral Expectations

How many specific student behaviors are we as teachers monitoring throughout a day?

- *How are students entering the classroom?*
- *How are they organizing their work space?*
- *How are they interacting with their peers?*

Such observations could be made for every student in our classroom within the first hour of the school day and tracked every hour after until the end of the school day, and still would only represent a fraction of possible behavioral observations. Yet, we do not track or record all of these behaviors. For the first few weeks of a school year, teachers may practice routines slowly throughout each day to ensure that we observe each student successfully move through each procedure. The goal those first few weeks is to have specific procedures practiced to the point of habit so that the rest of the year can move forward without the need to monitor those specific behaviors. Instead, what we do is practice these routines until they become habit and then monitor those behaviors that do not align with these practiced routines.

Such routines may involve monitoring specific student behaviors such as:

- *Lining up outside the door in a single file line, hands to the side, facing forward.*
- *Taking out your pencils, papers, and other materials you need for the day's lesson.*
- *When asked to share with a peer, waiting your turn to share and returning attention to the teacher when cued.*

I have observed the compliance of such classroom routines and a part of me is always impressed when a teacher is able to say a phrase, present a gesture, or stand in a particular spot in the classroom and have students respond with specific expected behaviors. Compliance is an impressive sight for outside observers and varying degrees of compliance for general behavior expectations exist across many classrooms. The intention for detailing this idea of compliance for general behavior expectations is to say that behaviors, generally, are being exercised by many students even though they are not being recorded and reported in writing by their teachers for the benefit of creating a particular academic learning environment.

Generally speaking, classrooms require students to behave in ways that may not be intuitive to them. This is a point for conversation that teachers will want to have in their Professional Learning Communities (PLCs) regarding their general expectations for behavior. Expectations for behavior must not be strictly age-appropriate—they must consider the developing social and emotional components of the students in each classroom as part of a larger school vision that supports a self-directed learning environment.

This is where it becomes critical for school staff to understand each social and emotional component well enough to be able to coach students in their own development of these skills. In order to coach these skills, we must learn to live by these social and emotional components in ways that align with our school's vision. This means that every general behavior expectation we set for students must intentionally address at least one social-emotional component in a way that aligns with a school's general behavior expectation for staff.

Look again at the prior examples of behavior expectations at the start of this section. Acknowledge that each may require a degree of compliance but that each may also link to a social-emotional component.

1. **How are students entering the classroom?** Lining up outside the door in a single file line, hands to the side, facing forward.

    SEL Component: *Societal Awareness: Responsibility (Rules and Consequences).* As adults, we often need to stand in lines out of both safety and respect for those that are also waiting for their opportunity to share in receiving particular goods and services.

2. **How are they organizing their work space?** Take out your pencils, papers, and other materials you need for the day's lesson.

    SEL Component: *Self-Awareness and Management: Self-Reflection and Goal-Setting.* Students who have set goals for the day, week, or month, will need to be aware of the steps needing consistent follow-through in order to achieve those goals. Students who do not have such resources may require a teacher or other sponsor to assist them in accomplishing such steps as part of their development in self-reflection and goal-setting.

3. **How are they interacting with their peers?** Wait your turn to share ideas and return attention when done.

   SEL Component: *Social-Awareness and Relationships: Interpersonal Skills.* Students benefit when they practice sharing their thoughts with peers in a way that prompts a listener to share their thoughts in return. Observing how students interact may give insight into how teachers may adjust their learning environment and practices to promote such skills through explicit instruction, modeling, and opportunities for exercising these skills.

Observation of all student behaviors need not be recorded daily, and it can be typical for teachers to record individual student behaviors that are *not* following general behavior expectations in the classroom. This is where behavioral coaching comes in to play, specifically in how teachers respond to such behaviors that fall outside of a classroom's general behavior expectations. It is important to note here that behaviors falling outside of general behavior expectations typically involve any student in any tier and that the social and emotional development of individual students across the tiers will need to be addressed according to their particular development rather than an age-based preset for grade level behavior expectations. To be clear, the focus here is on growth, more than it is on proficiency, over time, and it is this growth that we aspire to observe, record, and report.

Example: Coaching Self-Awareness and Management

I previously had a student in my class that would turn in an assignment with an error or needed revision and, upon providing guidance and advice, the student would inevitably respond with self-deprecating outrage, throwing her pencil on the floor, stomping back to her seat—always in tears. This was not a typical response for my fifth-grade classroom so it caught me off guard the first time it happened. I later went to speak to her prior year's teacher to discover that this was, unfortunately, typical for this student.

I considered what could be causing this extreme lack of self-confidence in the classroom. This student had positive support at home, had been observed having positive friends at school, but her image of herself still seemed to be negative. The next time I saw this student, I had a casual chat with her about the things she likes to do at school, at home, with her friends, and with her family. Her responses were short and did not provide much insight. There didn't seem to be a lot that she valued in herself (or at least wanted to share with me)—her self-efficacy was low and she had difficulty recognizing the role that mistakes play in the learning process.

When she would hand in an assignment, she would have a look on her face that seemed to anticipate her failed effort. I made a few attempts to highlight the aspects about her work that were excellent but she was not convinced and replied with a question regarding its grade and whether it's passing or failing. When I explained that revising only one or two parts will meet the academic standard, she would quickly take the paper and stomp back to her seat upset that her work was failing.

This went on much the same way as I tried a few other approaches, speaking with her outside of class, front-loading support before an assignment, giving advice during the time she worked on an assignment, and again providing feedback after an assignment is submitted, all with similar negative response. It wasn't until about three months into the school year that a similar interaction between her and I ended with her grabbing her paper out of my hands as she headed for the exit. I called for her to come back and firmly explained that leaving without me knowing where she will be going is not safe. I followed this up by saying that she must find a way to accept mistakes as part of learning. I pressed in that moment how important it is that she recognize how much she has accomplished in these past few months and that, with the support of her classmates, her family, her teachers, and the effort she continues to put in to her work, it is important that she recognize how amazingly hardworking and intelligent she is.

In that moment, she again started pointing out the mistakes on her assignment and for every mistake she claimed to exist, I pointed out each of her strengths. When she ran out of negatives to highlight, I asked her if she remembers learning to ride a bike and she silently nodded. I asked if she remembers jumping on the bike and speeding down the street right away or whether it took time, help from her parents, help from her friends, and confidence in herself to improve until she could finally ride on her own alongside her friends. She seemed to be genuinely considering this thought so I suggested she go get some water and come back to revise her work to meet the standard and resubmit the assignment.

While she was out of the room, I addressed the class as I felt the students needed an explanation since they were well aware of this particular student's reaction and the efforts that have been made to support her. I explained how we are all working on something, that self-directed learners are always struggling with a skill or a concept, that we as humans must recognize that we, as much as the person next to us, will need help in recognizing how awesome we are—every day—and to continue helping each other learn more today than we knew yesterday; to be proud of ourselves and of each other because we are all working hard and deserve to be reminded of this by our peers.

The student came back and the class went on for the rest of the day as it would normally. However, over the next several weeks, I began to notice small changes in her reactions to her peers. She would still be somewhat bothered by mistakes in her work but, around February of that school year, upon receiving my feedback on an assignment, explained in her own words (out loud!) that it's okay that she made a small mistake because it wouldn't take long for her to fix it and turn the assignment in again for full credit. By the end of the year, this student ended up having not only one of the highest academic scores across all state-required standardized assessments for the class but showed the largest growth in one year than any student in that class.

This particular story is meant to highlight how developing an awareness of self-efficacy not only means addressing individual student development but also recognizing the time it takes to develop in students this awareness of being self-directed and taking ownership of their own learning academically as well as socially and emotionally.

Example: Coaching Social-Awareness and Relationships

Recently, I had the opportunity to teach third grade and, two years later, fifth grade at the same school. I was fortunate that the majority of my third-grade students were my students once again. One of those students in particular had an IEP that included self-regulation as an area of need with accommodations that included suggestions for particular coping strategies. These strategies were to be incorporated into the instructional opportunities for this student and I couldn't be happier about it. Having an IEP officially list suggested coping strategies for a student was a wonderful surprise. It typically takes quite some time to discover which coping strategies work for my students! Because it was not a behavioral 504 plan, the strategies suggested broadly suggested coping strategies for particular behaviors which came to be an even better situation for me in developing my self-directed classroom.

When I began my fifth-grade year, during those first many weeks working through self-directed learning routines and practices, I incorporated deep breathing and meditation into the classroom learning environment. This allowed my student with an IEP to receive opportunities to practice these coping strategies herself and allowed for that strategy to be accessed within a learning environment that included other students who knew to recognize that strategy and be aware of its purpose and intent. Coping strategies became part of the students' conversations in the classroom as they would occasionally tell each other that they just have to take some deep breaths, step outside for a drink of water, and basically give each other space when they felt stressed. It was never a big show or long discussion but was enough for students in the class to be reminded that it was okay to take a minute for themselves to cope with a stressful day.

Although coping strategies themselves are a *Self-Awareness and Management* skill, it is the incorporation of these coping strategies within the classroom learning environment that made it so important that I coach students on how to share and support each other in using these strategies as a means for also developing *Social-Awareness and Relationships* skills.

I didn't introduce these coping strategies to students in the first week of school—I needed to develop not only my own trust in my students but also in my students trusting me. Coping strategies for students at schools that do not promote them school-wide requires an inordinate amount of trust within the walls of the classroom.

A recent dissertation by Lindsey S. Mantz of the University of Delaware in 2017 looked at the role of relationships and teaching with regard to school-based social-emotional development. On page 35 of her work, she explained how "students in classrooms with teachers who frequently model effective problem-solving, prosocial behavior, and appropriate interactions and relationships with others (and therefore have positive relationships with their students) are more likely to engage in prosocial and socially competent behaviors as well." This serves as an important point that studies are showing positive correlations between a teacher's ability to build relationships with their students and their students being able to also build positive relationships with others. This ties directly to my efforts in promoting coping strategies that, unbeknown to my students, were legally assigned as IEP accommodations for only one student. This meant that promoting prosocial and socially competent behaviors in order to cultivate a trusting learning environment through the use of effective emotional coping strategies required that I develop trust between me and my students. Ultimately, what resulted was (within my self-directed learning environment) a development of prosocial student behaviors that supported not only empathy in each other's ability to cope with stress but also practice in the interpersonal skills and conflict resolution due to students discussing their academic (and personal) concerns in order to support each other in meeting their academic (and personal) goals.

For the student with the IEP that included these coping strategies in her accommodations, the biggest takeaway is the fact that this example was not about her own ability to exercise coping skills but rather focused on my responsibility for coaching all students in developing coping strategies. This is also an example of how supporting behavior expectations of students from all tiers of my behavior model, including my students with IEPs, incorporates into my general behavior expectations the very strategies designed for one particular student in a way that supports all of my students.

Example: Coaching Societal Awareness

When I visit a community's local businesses and organizations, it doesn't take long to track down individuals that support developing students' SEL skills such as goal-setting, self-reflection, and interpersonal skills. A school's community will likely share values such as *hard work*, positive persistence, and practical problem solving. When it comes to in-class behavioral coaching, extending this to the community takes a little outreach and organizational planning to connect what students are learning in the classroom to their own community projects and businesses.

When it comes to the elementary grade levels, it is common to hold a *career day* or to visit a local fire station to see what's going on in a student's community. Having professionals come into the classroom and respond to student questions about their work in businesses and organizations within their own community is important for students to experience. This is where the lessons on why rules exist and the basis for self-management and relationships can be presented in contexts that give purpose to the SEL-related routines practiced in schools.

The most important part of coaching societal awareness in a classroom is the need for parental support of in-class behavioral coaching. Being clear on the skills you may be developing in your students will provide opportunities for parents to communicate back to you on progress and problems that not only benefit your efforts in the classroom but also extend what you are coaching in your classroom to the community outside of your classroom's four walls— this remains true across all grade levels.

There was a year when I taught all subjects for a sixth and seventh grade as a combination class at a brand new charter school—I was the sole middle school teacher that first year. There were a few parents and school staff that had some amazing professional connections and it was not difficult for me to provide students with opportunities to take what we were learning in class and extend it to the community. There was a community theater down the road where a school staff member served as a sponsor for a theatre troupe. We were offered an opportunity to experience a live theatrical performance during the months that I was teaching concepts related to theatrical performance. The ability to review with my students the importance of sitting quietly out of respect for performers on stage, when to applaud (and when not to), and to be aware of the fact that these actors worked really hard to learn all of their lines and follow their blocking in order to create what was happening in front of the students. This all really sunk in once my students had a chance to meet the actors before the performance and discuss with the actors how they felt before, during, and after a performance. My students got to ask questions such as how long they'd been doing this, and the like.

The most compelling example that promotes the need for coaching societal awareness in the classroom is a conversation I had with a family friend that works for a company that cultivates culture in large companies and organizations. The conversation was based in the idea that companies are seeking motivated workers that not only follow directions but also are able to work collaboratively, speak well across a company's hierarchy, and provide insight and solutions to unexpected problems. Employers of large companies look to hire those that not only can identify problems and solutions but also can critically examine resolutions that, though they may not seem equal, maximize benefits of all parties involved (e.g., Flood-Dresher Experiment). When I suggested to this family friend that their company or companies they support actively engage and assist in developing these skills in community schools, the reaction was very positive. This potential for schools and teachers willing and able to recognize and develop in students these SEL components that high-profile companies are seeking may have an opportunity to not only cultivate a more meaningful approach to social and emotional learning but also give value to middle and high school students exercising these strategies.

The most difficult aspect of coaching this particular area (societal awareness) of social and emotional development is in recognizing the inevitable push-back on specific industry values in today's changing world. It is important to maintain a global perspective on the cultivation of values that does not strictly support one industry (e.g., business finance, insurance, real estate) over another (e.g., construction, agriculture, mining).

I recently attended a conference that featured a presentation on globalizing the classroom through technology. The focus was on middle and high school classrooms through the use of online platforms that promote global citizenship and real-world problem solving through global collaboration. One of the platforms discussed was iEARN which promotes "learning with the world, not just about it" by hosting an International Education and Resource Network. With over one hundred active projects every year, this global community of educators and students collaborates on projects focused on humanities and social sciences, language and storytelling, as well as science, technology, engineering, and math, aligned with seventeen United Nations Sustainable Development Goals for the 2017–2018 academic year.

As students become older with each grade level, they become more inclined to find interest in the social aspects of their lives. Taking the opportunity to coach students in expanding their concept of social structures in the context of their responsibilities as global citizens will only be limited by the opportunities presented or allowed by the classroom teacher. It is this perspective that is important for schools to keep in mind as they cultivate in their teachers a desire to develop all SEL competencies in all grade levels as appropriate, but most definitely the self-awareness and management skills in elementary school students, social-awareness and relationship skills in middle school students, and societal awareness in high school students.

Behavioral coaching in a behavioral inclusive environment requires the teacher to not only take on the inclusivity of academic progress across a wide range of students but also the inclusivity of social and emotional progress across that same wide range of students. To those that consider this an impossible task, I say it is not impossible—it is something many teachers are already doing and are only in need of a framework for identifying these observations. I am currently designing a framework for this purpose but, for now, it is important to recognize that the particular needs of each student takes time to observe and monitor behavior patterns. It is for this reason that behavioral coaching is a secondary concept that benefits from a solid understanding in social-emotional learning as well as cognitive and psychosocial development. This allows teachers to not only account for the academic growth according to content-related responses to assigned tasks but also the social and emotional growth according to interactions within the classroom that the teachers in the room can observe, record, and assist students in meaningful reflection over time.

BEHAVIORAL INTERVENTION [SCHOOL-WIDE APPROACH]

The intent of a school-wide behavioral intervention program is in response to the small percentage of ineffective results from in-class behavioral coaching. When teachers are implementing a consistent approach to in-class behavioral coaching (whether from a purchased program or developed in-house), there will likely be a reasonable boundary of general behavior expectations that the majority of students across all tiers are able to meet as they improve their SEL skill sets throughout their academic career. Many students will benefit from in-class behavioral coaching to meet and reflect on these general behavioral expectations. A small percentage of students might fall below the boundary of general behavioral expectations to the point where in-class behavioral coaching is not proving effective. It is for these students that a school-wide approach to explicit instruction and ongoing reflection of SEL skills may be most beneficial.

Behavior Expectations

Use Kind Words   Follow Directions

Respect Property and Persons   Seek Help and Solve Problems

Behavioral Intervention

Self-Awareness   Self-Efficacy   Self-Reflection

Empathy & Perspective   Interpersonal Skills   Conflict Resolution

Societal Responsibility   Community Building

Punitive Measures*

School-Wide Restorative Practices

Committee for Individual Suspension or Expulsion

(Measures based on school policy and state ed code.)

This illustration highlights the need of a school-wide approach for behavioral intervention to have a structure that promotes a positive progression toward meeting general behavior expectations.

It has been my experience that teachers will remove a student from a class-room after several attempts to get the student on track so that learning may continue in the classroom. Once a student is removed from a class-room, the specific steps in place for managing that student will differ from school to school based on both a school's philosophy as well as available resources and staffing. However, some aspects of such next steps will be consistent across campuses depending on whether a school has a punitive or reflective approach.

Most schools have a flow chart of consequences that provide transparency to teachers, students, and parents about common behaviors that are handled in the classroom, patterns of behavior that require parent contact, and behav-iors that require immediate administrative intervention (with room for spe-cial cases and anomalies). The consequences for these behaviors are typically listed with varying degrees of detail in a school-issued parent handbook.

The suggestions for behavioral intervention in this section is organized by approach for lower elementary, upper elementary, and middle/high school to account for the cognitive and psychosocial development of each range of grade levels. It may be that an upper elementary range includes third through fifth or third through sixth, and a middle school range may include sixth through eighth or seventh through ninth. The goal isn't to delineate accord-ing to specific ages or grade levels but rather by development of the students. With this in mind, please consider the following approaches with a develop-mental mindset.

Early Elementary Behavioral Intervention

What is most important to understand about behavior intervention in the early elementary grade levels is that much of the behaviors outside of the various student tiers will likely be the result of those years of development leading up to the early elementary school years. The focus for a teacher's behavior intervention will likely involve coordination with their school's special education team to tease out possible development cues that can be structured into individual student's daily routines.

Behavioral intervention at the elementary ages, especially that of early ele-mentary, takes into consideration the series of developmental stages crucial for teachers to understand when seeking to intervene and provide support for a young student. Even though a student, depending on their age, may or may not have worked through certain stages, understanding that a stu-dent might have developed shame or doubt in their abilities may have an effect on their ability to initiate productive behaviors. This effect may look different in another student who developed a strong sense of autonomy and initiative. These differences in development are the types of things a teacher may want to discuss with their special education team in order to have a meaningful conversation with colleagues about productive interven-tion supports for students unwilling (or unable) to meet general behavior expectations. It is also reasonable for teachers to discuss with their special education team the particular behaviors they may want to note in order to determine which student actions should be recorded through this lens of seeking behavioral intervention.

As students move up through first and second grade, they will have transitioned (or will be transitioning) into a stage of industry versus inferiority. This stage lasts up through middle school, so it is crucial that this stage be fully understood and implemented in a classroom's behavioral coaching and inclusion models. The difference when it comes to intervention now becomes what concepts students are cognitively able to understand. Around the ages of six and seven, students begin to understand and question the logic of teachers, parents, and their peers.

However, the hypothetical depth of such concepts as fairness, injustice, love, and respect is often lost on lower elementary grade level students. From a social-emotional perspective, lessons of empathy and interpersonal skills will require experience and in-the-moment reflection for these ideas to be internalized and developed. It is important to consider, although students may be able to repeat back complex words that represent abstract ideas, it will be through the use of role-playing and active participation that students internalize the value of these concepts.

In a March 2019 NPR report, "Teaching Kids to Control Their Anger," anthropologist Jean Briggs is credited for her observation of a family interaction in the Canadian Arctic while studying Inuit culture. Her observation details a mother taking her two-year-old son and prompting the child to throw a pebble very hard at her. When the kid does as he was told, the mother exclaimed in pain how much it hurt.

> The parent then asks a question to keep the child thinking about the consequences, like, don't you like me?—the implication being that hitting hurts people's feelings. The parents keep putting on these little plays from time to time until the child learns not to hit. Myna grew up learning from these types of dramas. She says these plays also teach kids to keep their cool ... You can do it with a drama, a story or grab two stuffed animals and act it out. She says just make sure you keep the tone fun and playful. She says many parents forget how powerful play is in disciplining and sculpting kids' behavior. (Doucleff, 2019)

This NPR story is relevant in that it relays how important play is at these early elementary years. It is also important to note that the quotes supporting the story are from psychologists at Northeastern University and New York City. If children at these early ages are behaving in ways that are actively and continuously disrupting the learning in a classroom, it may be necessary to emphasize the language for emotional reactions to behaviors through play. Strengthening awareness of all students in the classroom will benefit the few that are struggling with these ideas. It will be equally important to include the parents to ensure that efforts within the school are being mirrored in the home.

It will be helpful to target specific behaviors to be intervened within a social-emotional framework. The November 2018 article in Prevention Science, "The Core Components of Evidence-Based Social Emotional Learning Programs," suggests that identifying core SEL components "may inform training programs and quality indicators" and includes a list of behavior indicators that align with SEL competencies according to the percentage frequency each behavior indicator appears in a variety of SEL programs (Lawson, McKenzie, Becker, Selby, & Hoover, 2018). If a student shows difficulty in a behavior such as "identifying feelings based on face and body cues, and context", this article suggests that most SEL programs could provide meaningful intervention for this particular skill. However, if a student shows difficulty in "differentiating between thoughts, feelings, and behaviors", this article suggests that few SEL programs could provide meaningful intervention.

Upper Elementary Behavioral Intervention

At the upper elementary grade levels, behavioral intervention will fall somewhere between the lower elementary and the middle and high school approach. The biggest difference is the explanations and contexts of reasoning provided to students as they develop strategies that meet the school's general behavior expectations.

For the student who is not able to adapt to a teacher's in-class behavioral coaching and continues to consistently disrupt student learning, that student may require one-on-one time before school to chat about what they plan to do during the day. During that time, it is also important to listen to specific questions, topics, activities, interests, and collect information on how that student thinks about themselves and their environment. This initial approach to individualized intervention targets the executive functioning skills that can be monitored daily and reflected upon at the end of each week. The struggle is dependent on resources and staffing available based on how many students are in need of such intervention.

These brief chats may involve students who seem to use very simple words to describe increasingly complicated situations. For these students, it may help to refer to words for feelings related to both simple as well as compound emotions in order to assist the student in describing a potential increase in difficult social situations. For students who are frustrated with their own ability to be good at something in academics, social circles, sports, and the like, it may help to refer to goal-setting strategies specific to what the student is trying to accomplish. For students who constantly focus their conversations on what other students think of them, it might be helpful to refer to their own self-efficacy and what makes them feel proud, or perhaps discussing interpersonal skills such as things people say and do to join groups and feel welcome.

These are all limited examples of the kinds of topics behavioral intervention might include. The time spent listening to students is designed to give those students an outlet that they otherwise may be expressing as a disruption during classroom learning time. This also offers an opportunity for teachers to hear how their students might prefer to pursue goals, both academic and social, that they otherwise might feel are out of reach. For my part, providing a sounding board that helps students strategize steps to meet a goal, not only helps them organize their own thoughts and gives them positive affirmation of their efforts, it also helps me to monitor student efforts while I am addressing my class through behavioral coaching.

In my experience, the majority of behavioral intervention is largely handled within these sessions and rarely requires involvement by administration. It is important to provide insight with school resource personnel such as site counselors and school or district psychologists regarding approaches to intervention sessions. It is also critical to communicate with parents regarding student behaviors and intervention progress in order to promote mirroring of general behavior expectations at home as well as in the classroom.

In the event that a large enough group of upper elementary students are in need of a weekly group session, the approach may become more similar to the middle and high school approach.

Middle and High School Behavioral Intervention

What is described in this section is support for implementing the idea described at the end of this chapter (see: *When Brute Force Fails*).

Behavioral intervention at the middle and high school ages, especially that of the middle school ages, takes into consideration a critical transition between two of Erikson's psychosocial stages of development. During the middle school years, students are beginning to consider a new crisis of identity versus role confusion. It is common to associate this transition with puberty as it applies to physical changes and needs, but this perspective focuses more on the idea of puberty as it relates to the development of more complex emotions that are inherent in the situations in which these students may find themselves. Students may experience an increase in desired approval of peers, defining their role within peer-based social structures, and an influence of peers suddenly greater than the influence of parents and teachers. It is important for students to begin identifying these psychosocial changes and increasing their vocabulary for discussing complex emotions that may build up more rapidly due to this increase in social awareness. It will also be important for students to begin recognizing coping strategies for dealing with increasing emotions without serious damage to themselves or others. It is important for these students to recognize the value in their own interests, value in goal-setting and perseverance, value in empathy and friendships, as well as the value of their actions and reactions as they affect those around them.

The most important difference to be considered is in student cognitive development for middle and high school age students. During these years, students develop what Piaget refers to as the Formal Operational stage. This stage of hypothetical reasoning incorporates abstract and cross-concept logic. In the middle school ages, this transition can be confusing to students who might be seeking to apply this type of logic to situations that may not be necessary or find such logic difficult to maneuver in increasingly complex contexts. Student frustrations can result from a developed sense of inferiority, guilt, or doubt in their own abilities due to experiences from the prior ten years of their life and, as these students consistently disrupt learning in the classroom, may not recognize that their sudden shift in attitude may be a natural defense mechanism that they can learn to develop and control in productive ways.

Schools that efficiently track misbehaviors are at an advantage in identifying not only the most frequently disruptive students but the behaviors most frequently causing the disruptions. Whether a school tracks the various types of behaviors (e.g., in-class behavior, out-of-class behavior, removing students from classrooms, or any number of specific behaviors) that fall outside of a school's general behavior expectations, the data collected can provide helpful information on which students may need targeted behavioral intervention. The most helpful information to collect is the frequency and quality of disruptions, but with more emphasis on the quantity over the quality of the disruption.

For example, if a student uses profanity to express general frustration several times a week, they may receive several notices of misbehavior throughout a given week. Contrast that against another student who profanely and explosively finds fault with another student (or teacher) in anger; the quality of such an event may be marked as equal to that of the first student who repeatedly uses casual swearing with no malintent. Comparing these two examples, both students may be viewed through an end-of-week analysis of behavioral data as equally disruptive students. However, I would argue that the student with a record of high-frequency disruptions of profanity is of much more concern because the disruptions are overriding efforts by the classroom teacher and their peers to remedy that specific behavior. However, the student with a single disruption involving targeted profanity may be a single misbehavior that only requires a brief discussion to resolve a single targeted issue.

Schools that track misbehaviors are also at an advantage in the distribution of school resources toward behavioral intervention. My thought here is that the majority of what are considered a school's *punitive* resources need be directed toward that smallest percentage of students with the highest frequency of repeated misbehaviors. When combined with the idea that a teacher's resources are focused on in-class behavioral coaching, both ideas can work in tandem to increase the chance that classroom learning environments can improve. This concept is intended to replace the approach of addressing all misbehaviors equally regardless of quantity and quality.

Schools and teachers that have effective behavior data will want to begin a specific strategy for behavioral intervention that is specific to the students' needs. Be wary of prepurchased programs intended for any students in any school. It is important for teachers, parents, and administrators to recognize that the behavior intervention model applied must follow the development of social and emotional learning that the school is promoting and that it is considered a possibility that middle and high school students in need of behavioral intervention be started at the earliest stages of social-emotional development.

The most important similarity between the elementary and middle/high school levels is that the smallest percentage of highest frequency misbehaving students are to be addressed.

Ideas for Behavioral Intervention

It may seem like there are an infinite number of approaches and ideas to consider when introducing social-emotional learning to a behavioral intervention environment.

This first idea is good for both in-class behavioral coaching as well as behavioral intervention. It is a perspective that considers when and how we learn about *rules* as students and why consequences exist for students who haven't internalized the ideas inherent in those rules.

It begins with a line at the bottom of a page that represents the bottom-line *rules and consequences* associated with a school's framework of values. I use a metaphor that compares students to birds that find themselves standing on this line, this hard floor, and that when they trip and fall, to them, it hurts because they've only ever fallen that short distance. How the other birds treat each other when things like this happen matters because pretty soon the birds will learn to fly. As birds begin to learn to fly, mistakes in flight may cause them to fall back down to that same ground which they will discover now hurts just a little bit more. How other birds look after each other and learn to fly together matters because when one bird makes a mistake in flight, that bird will want the rest to help keep them from hitting that ground. During this time, while still relatively close to the ground, these birds will take risks perhaps to challenge other birds' ability to fly, and occasionally they will fall as well. It is important that the other birds recognize this behavior as exercising the existence of those rules and boundaries according to their increased ability to fly in an expanding environment. Eventually, each bird will learn to fly higher and closer to the clouds, upward into altitudes and environments that incorporate increasing challenges (and more incredible views, e.g., intrinsic rewards). The lessons they learned closer to the ground will help them to fly to greater heights, to broaden their world view, and meet more birds that can help them explore other interesting environments. Mistakes in flight at these upward heights will always be a risk that could result in a bird falling so far as to hit that same hard ground. The higher the bird is flying, the more that ground will hurt.

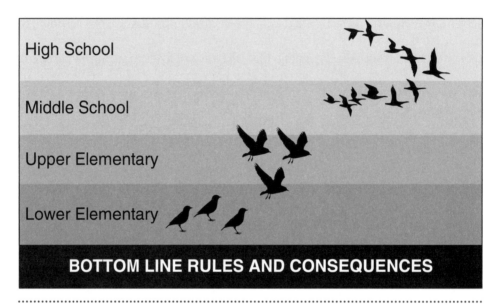

High School

Middle School

Upper Elementary

Lower Elementary

BOTTOM LINE RULES AND CONSEQUENCES

SOURCE: Bird images courtesy of Pixabay.

While this may seem an inappropriate analogy for children, it is not a shock or surprise to students who have had family and friends in their own communities involved in illegal activities that have resulted in unfortunate circumstances. In my experience, students as early as second grade have been open about their experiences with similar events. This analogy not only describes a perspective toward student reciprocity and peer-based support but also is an approach to a classroom management style that recognizes these various stages of metaphorical flight as grade levels and that if students do not learn to fly together when they are closer to that ground, it will begin to hurt more the higher they are expected to fly. This puts a greater emphasis on the teacher's role as a behavioral coach to help students recognize this perspective and support them in learning how to work with each other in order to build a more positive peer-based learning environment.

This next idea is one I use for students who seem to have trouble empathizing or connecting with other students. I target the development of leadership in students who may show strong signs of emotional awareness and strong cognitive capacity (academic growth). By addressing leadership abilities in these few students, I am able to not only curb social distress among these students but also build an awareness and acceptance that helps these students understand the behaviors of others.

For these students who may have consistent minor behaviors but no significant pattern of intense negative classroom behavior, I will explain to them what it means to be *a leader*. By focusing on these aspects of a leader and explaining to them that they have in them the ability to lead, I can harness their outgoing energy in developing something they want—attention and self-worth. The trick here is that being a leader takes practice, that practice takes time, and that even leaders will make decisions not everybody likes. How leaders handle these difficult situations and make these decisions is exactly what makes them a leader. This process takes several weeks of meeting once or twice a week during recess or lunch. I find that most students I invite to participate in this are more than willing. With these sessions, I am able to instill in them deeper understanding of empathy and go over their own reactions to specific scenarios and situations they may experience. This allows me to develop in these students a trust in the classroom that becomes a positive force for helping other students since these students are already the outgoing talkative students who may already be trying to help their peers.

HOW TO BE A LEADER

1. **Show respect to those around you (even when you don't feel like it).** Recognize the good in every person—even people that are not respectful to you. Showing respect to all people shows trust and leadership.

2. **Communicate (in a way that not only informs, but inspires).** "Leadership is the art of getting someone else to do something you want done because he wants to do it." – D. Eisenhower

3. **Be generous (with time, encouragement, and responsibility).** Encourage others by focusing on how they can grow. Praise a person's growth and they will soon meet higher expectations.

4. **Express your passion (because that's how passion spreads).** Be proud of things you like and share your joy with others. This will encourage others to share the joy in what they like.

5. **Be humble (this doesn't mean being a pushover).** As a leader, people are already inspired by your success. Be proud of your accomplishments and know you are already seen as a leader.

6. **Be decisive (and take responsibility for your decisions).** Tough decisions may make some people unhappy. Help the most people possible and help others understand your decision.

7. **Show courage (even when you're scared).** Leaders can be afraid but still have the courage to do what will help the most people.

SOURCE: Adapted from DeMers, 2014.

Another resource is a cost-benefit approach toward the value of school and *being a student* seen here with the following four-column chart.

GOAL	COST	DISTRACTION	BENEFIT
What are you here to achieve and why is this goal important?	*What are you willing to spend to achieve your goal?*	*Who and what can stop you from achieving your goal?*	*What is the value of the costs apart from achieving your goal?*

This resource by itself can be completed quickly at a glance with minimal effect, but with the right approach can be very powerful. The resource itself is only a blank white paper with four columns and a line at the top for column headings. I guide students to write the word *goals* in the left-most column heading followed by a brief discussion where students write down what goals they have (e.g., professional soccer player, college, a job, raising their own kids). In the second column heading, students are to write the word *costs* followed by a brief discussion where students write down the various things students must do in a classroom and what that costs them being a student (e.g., time to sleep and play, pride in asking to use the restroom, respect in doing what other people tell me to do, money for supplies). I will typically provide other more abstract ideas to consider such as being punctual, caring for other students, and paying attention to what others are saying. I skip the third column at this point and have students write in the fourth heading the word *benefits* followed by a brief discussion where students write the things they expect to receive in return for being a student (e.g., good grades, college, job) and I often provide considerations that are more abstract such as success, trust, friends, and the like.

Back to that third column, I have students write the word *distractions* followed by a brief discussion where students write down the things that, if the costs were worth spending to receive those benefits, and if those benefits were valuable enough to equal the costs lists, what distractions exist now that might stop them from receiving those benefits. This third column is the game changer for an otherwise simple activity. This turns the activity away from me as a teacher guiding them through a worksheet and putting all emphasis of the activity's value on their own personal lives. I typically do not have students write down these distractions and offer this column as optional, especially if I intend to collect them for my own review and reflection as the teacher running the behavioral intervention.

The hard-hitting reality of this activity, specifically for middle and high school students is that this idea of cost and benefit is appealing to them and the visual representation of their own life's distractions stopping them from receiving benefits due to a question of value of cost attributed to their own behaviors is one that they have likely not considered. It seems to resonate with students at the middle and high school ages not only because of its hypothetical nature but also because it relates to the control they have over their own lives. It uses words they have heard before and puts them into the context of their own behaviors and the connection those words have to the benefits they desire. It is a simple idea that they have never sat down and thought through with this level of mindfulness which makes it a powerful tool during an initial intervention setting.

These few examples of resources and approaches are not designed as a single one-time intervention *quick fix* for students. These examples are to show how behavioral intervention can put into perspective many different components of Social-Emotional Learning that may not explicitly state any one component. The concept of behavioral intervention requires an understanding of Social-Emotional Learning that can get at the heart of those students who represent the smallest percentage causing the highest percentage of frustration for teachers and their peers. When a school can help these few students figure out why they are at school and the value of being a student, then work on developing the skills that other students will value in return, classroom learning environments will improve and that high percentage of teacher and peer frustration will begin to dip.

When Brute Force Fails

There is one last idea to suggest on the basis that some classrooms may have a variety of students who violate various rules each week and that addressing them all with equal resources and attention is an unrealistic expectation. The professional judgment of a classroom teacher must account for the distribution of justice according to the severity of student misbehaviors. The following is an idea that has been applied in cities around the United States in similar situations and is being adapted to the conditions related to general school campuses.

First and foremost, prioritize student misbehaviors within a classroom not by severity but by quantity and reassign the highest percentage of resources, time, and commitment to ongoing SEL intervention for those students who have a record of repeat misbehaviors over several weeks (or months). When I ask teachers to tell me how many students in their classroom are responsible for the majority of disruptions in the classroom, the number is generally a single digit. When I ask teachers across classrooms in similar grade levels, I typically hear many of the same student names from various teachers. For this reason, treating these students with the same consequences as other students with far fewer infractions or significantly less severe incidents is ineffective. The students with only a few entries of misbehavior, regardless of severity, are not the ongoing cause of an entire learning environment being disrupted. The focus of resources, time, and commitment from the teachers must not be equal for the student who is returning to the same environment where their misbehavior can continue without reflection or regard for their peers.

This idea to reassign resources is intended to provide increased structure that may not be necessary for the majority of students in the same classroom. This is not to say that the majority of students are not breaking rules but teachers must address the discrepancy between breaking a rule due to a minor upset that is handled quickly and respectfully and the breaking of a rule that continually stops the learning of others from happening.

Some ways in which a teacher can help structure the day for these students:

- Require students to check in to ensure they have what they need for the day
- Individual weekly chats to receive updates on how things are going
- Monthly parent phone calls to receive updates on how things are going

Again, these are not one-time *quick-fix* type intervention approaches. The creativity involved in addressing the needs of students with patterns of repeat misbehaviors takes time. The suggestions above may not even apply for students that refuse to show up on time or have families that do not respond to school outreach efforts. However, the teacher that does recognize the need for these students to have structure provided will more likely see the behaviors of those students change within the boundaries of their academic classroom and potentially in the interactions between them and their peers.

I have experience in this approach as I implemented a brief intervention program for middle school students who addressed this idea of focused intervention at a K–12 campus. I asked the middle school teachers to send me a list of students who are causing the most disruptions in their classrooms. Lo and behold, the result was a short list of similar names from each of the teachers. With the support of the middle school administration, I asked the teachers of those students to have a zero-tolerance policy for those students and to send them to my classroom at any point in the day whenever any of those students disrupts student learning. In return, those students would need to meet with me once a week after school for an hour to discuss various SEL competencies. The students were more excited than the teachers about this.

Immediately, teachers began sending students to my classroom (I was teaching an upper elementary grade level at the time). Students would be sent down for the smallest misbehaviors due to the zero-tolerance nature of the deal so some were bothered at the injustice initially. When I had them working with my upper elementary students, I would coach them on how to work with them, how to speak with them, how to help them. They would work with me and my students for about ten or fifteen minutes and I would send them back to class with a suggestion for coping with whatever caused them to react the way they did and disrupt the class.

Each week, those students would meet after school and talk about their week and discuss a particular SEL competency with me. It took a few weeks before they began to see the value of these after school discussions and reflect on the impact they were having on their social interactions.

After about three months, at least half of those students were no longer being sent to my room during the day. I would ask them why I haven't seen them and their answer would be some variant of, "I don't know, I'm not getting in trouble." Still, nearly half of the students would continue to be sent to me and only a few eventually suspended or expelled.

As I bring this section to a close, I would like to say that I believe all students deserve in-depth instruction and support of Social-Emotional Learning and that behavioral coaching can be extremely effective when infused in the general education classrooms. However, for those students who seem to fall outside of the general behavior expectations, and beyond the reach of in-class behavioral coaching, behavioral intervention provides those students an opportunity to really get into how Social-Emotional Learning is not a catchphrase as much as it is an understanding of their own self, social, and societal awareness. When students are in their classrooms, they will begin to see how social and emotional components are threaded into a teacher's in-class behavioral coaching style, and that their peers' attempts to work with them are seen as academic reciprocation that will benefit them and all other students in the classroom.

CHAPTER 6

Academic Inclusion and Intervention

When Standards-Based Learning and Cognitive and Psychosocial Development overlap, they create a secondary concept: Academic Inclusion and Intervention. This concept addresses the students whose academic growth and proficiency fall outside a reasonable range of general expectations for academic instruction and assessment.

A concept that is growing in popularity across the United States is referred to as a "Full Inclusion" model, Inclusive Education, or Full Inclusion Program. For the purpose of this chapter, Full Inclusion will be addressing the range of students who fall close to the range of students already struggling academically but may also have minor learning disabilities. Consider how Standards-Based Learning provides transparent academic expectations and proficiency levels. Consider also how SEL lends itself to the secondary concept of Self-Directed Learning and what effect that can have on a teacher's ability to monitor and provide support for those students who may need it most. Now combine that with specific theories of Cognitive and Psychosocial Development, the need for students to develop their sense of *industry versus inferiority* in elementary and middle school, and *identity versus role confusion* in middle and high school, and you uncover a meaningful purpose for an inclusive approach that can be expanded to meet the cognitive and psychosocial needs of all students, including those with an IEP.

It has been and continues to be my experience that any grade level I am assigned to teach has students who, although they are about the same age, are not at the same academic and social-emotional developmental levels. It is surprising only to those that are not classroom teachers that my classroom can have students who range from three- to six-year differences in ability, if not more. This means my third-grade class may have students reading at a kindergarten level and others at a fifth-grade level, some still skip counting while others working with algebraic concepts. The same goes for middle school and high school classrooms which may see even wider ranges of student proficiency in various academic skills. Because of such ranges of student ability in this age-based system of grade levels, I see the value in schools adopting a full inclusion model in combination with a standards-based approach supporting such wide ranges of student ability and growth. I see this as a productive step in preparing those responsible for improving schools including teachers, administrators, and policymakers, to consider adopting a full inclusion model.

ACADEMIC INCLUSION

My main argument for adopting a model that supports academic inclusion is the need for continuous adaptation as part of the developmental mindset (see page 58). For the purpose of this chapter, this mindset will consider the average human's cognitive and psychosocial development of school age children between the ages of around five to seventeen to align with the typical K–12 education schedule in the United States.

According to the theories of Piaget and Erikson, students who enter kindergarten at around five years of age are at a cognitive transition between Piaget's Preoperational and Concrete Operational stages and are about to enter Erikson's stage of Industry versus Inferiority. By eighth grade, those students will have reached the end of Piaget's Concrete Operational stage and transitioned into Piaget's Formal Operational stage, as well as reaching the end of Erikson's stage of Industry versus Inferiority and transitioning into Erikson's stage of Identity versus Role Confusion. This means that students, between the grade levels of kindergarten and eighth grade, are developing and transitioning through two sets of critical developmental stages. This also highlights some rationale for those teachers that seem to struggle in middle school classrooms. What I intend to describe is a rationale for inclusive differentiation, its use in a standards-based learning environment, and the means for identifying support for the various needs of students in a Full Inclusion model. As I describe this rationale, it is important to keep the following in mind that "success for students with special needs is determined individually by all members of the IEP team to determine if inclusive schooling is a benefit for that individual child" (McCarty, 2006).

DIFFERENTIATION FOR AN INCLUSIVE MODEL

First, it is important to recognize how a differentiated classroom might be defined. Carol Ann Tomlinson, in her 2014 book *The Differentiated Classroom*, says this about differentiation:

> Differentiated classrooms support students who learn in different ways and at different rates and who bring to school different

talents and interests . . . Teachers in differentiated classrooms are more in touch with their students and approach teaching more as an art than as a mechanical exercise. (p. 13)

I appreciated this perspective by Carol Ann Tomlinson and would agree that teaching is more of an art than a mechanical exercise in so much as it is seen as a balance of the two. The mechanical exercise of managing a classroom for the purpose of providing differentiated learning opportunities is what creates the autonomous self-directed learning environment by which teachers can artfully observe and differentiate that environment according to specific student needs.

I had the pleasure of meeting and speaking with Carol at a recent conference where she mentioned a wonderful analogy that she had heard from a musical colleague of hers. I'm paraphrasing here but the general idea is this: melody is the instruction for which the curriculum provides accompaniment. I noted that particular analogy as I am also a musician that greatly appreciated the depth behind that idea. In an attempt to see how far that analogy could go, I considered differentiation as the fusion of musical genres. I thought classical accompaniment may be too rigid for many of the students in our classrooms today and jazz may also be too out of touch. I liked the application of this idea with hip-hop not only because it is current but that the freedom of the lyrical flow of student ideas depends so much on the structure of the beat provided—the accompaniment (the beat) is the curriculum for which the melody of instruction (lyrical flow) can improvise.

This analogy helps me personally consider my own capacity for providing differentiated opportunities that support how my particular students may learn best; this is also as far as I am willing to take this analogy because it is through my own capacity for providing opportunities that I can allow for students to flow within the boundaries of the classroom learning environment. This means that differentiated practices such as flexible seating, lighting, music, alternative assessments and projects, multi-sensory activities, custom teacher instructional videos, journal reflection tasks, literature circles (book clubs), weekly *genius hour* sessions, mixed learning style groups, leveled proficiency tasks, learning stations (with or without mandatory rotations)—these opportunities are limited only by my willingness to provide a structure in which students are able to engage and improvise those opportunities intended to improve their own mastery of grade-level skills.

The biggest obstacle, in my experience, that a differentiated classroom addresses is the wide ranges of student ability levels within an age-based grade level classroom. The concern here is not only the wide range of student ability but more the approach to setting academic expectations for students who are more than a year or two behind (or ahead) in one or more academic subjects. When a seventh-grade teacher is presented a student reading at a third-grade level, the grade-level academic expectations are unreasonable expectations for this student. Now add to this challenge an awareness of cognitive and psychosocial ranges of development for these students and you can expect overwhelming frustration from the teachers as well as the students due to the differences between the expectations and ability.

To put this challenge into a reasonable perspective, first consider a lower elementary student who is excited to show how industrious they can be, is cognitively able to work with higher-order thinking skills and showing clear signs they are ready to be challenged academically, but prefers texts that are appropriate for the lower elementary grade levels. Reading an age-appropriate story such as one of a talking animal that works through a challenge and learns a lesson may be appropriate for meeting this child where they are emotionally but the academic assessments that may already be created for that story are too simple for this child. In this case, it would be reasonable for a teacher to provide opportunities for this student to discuss the character development of the talking animal as it relates to the impact the story's events have on that animal's world. It is important to recognize that this approach to differentiating the academic expectations to challenge this student at their ability level takes time and energy on the part of the teacher to provide those opportunities for that one student but is important in addressing academic differentiation in a way that supports a self-directed learning environment.

Now let's bring back that seventh-grade student reading at a third-grade level (four years below grade level according to age-based grade-level standards). Imagine that this student has spent the past four school years being decreasingly less industrious and increasingly unable to access the grade-level texts. Perhaps this student has shown a preference for more concrete texts and basic recall assessment questions. Perhaps the student's vocabulary and reading fluency is at a proficiency equal to a third- or fourth-grade level. This student may be turning to his friends for solace and escape from grade-level academic expectations as they work through their own crisis of identity. Teachers that are assessing this student according to grade-level academic expectations will inevitably mark this student with low academic scores that perhaps are causing the student to fall further behind emotionally as well as academically. This is a more challenging situation and, unfortunately, one that is more common in schools today.

So, what's the answer? Is there a quick-fix for teachers to solve this kind of problem within a single academic year? Is there a grab-and-go handbag of strategies to address these types of student needs? I believe the developmental mindset provides educators the means for identifying the strategies that address the particular obstacles in their classrooms, across their campuses, and in their communities.

In the following paragraphs, I will be describing only those aspects of an academic inclusion model that I have experience implementing. This limited aspect is due to the fact that there are many books on Full Inclusion models that go into great depths on the topic. My experience is in extending

Standards-Based Grading practices to include all students in my classroom based on a deeper understanding of cognitive and psychosocial development. Any overlap of my experience with that of other books on the subject is strictly coincidental and I encourage readers to explore other books and literature related to this topic.

STANDARDS-BASED DIFFERENTIATION

A standards-based model tracks student progress according to specific academic standards. Because I am able to assign specific levels of proficiency for each standard, I am also able to adapt tasks at proficiency levels that meet specific needs of my students. By setting a specific level of proficiency to standards, I am able to then provide series of tasks that develop specific students' ability to meet an expected level of proficiency. This is where a standards-based approach to differentiation can be most useful. Widening my ability to academically differentiate for any student who enters my class can be overwhelming at first.

Consider the aspects of a standards-based approach: standards, proficiency, assessments, resources, and reporting. It is our mastery of academic standards that prepares us to know how we can adjust formative and summative tasks to meet student needs. It is our own thorough understanding of the various depths of proficiency that allows us to adjust tasks as students develop throughout the year. Our own organization of classroom resources targeting specific standards helps me to direct students toward tasks that will provide support to meet student needs. This all connects as I adjust assessments I have made or purchased. It is all of these aspects together that supports the widening of my ability to differentiate in response to the fluid academic development of my students. These aspects will be presented as five targeted sections: Select the Skill (Standard); Prepare the Concept; Develop the Tasks; Practice: Prompt and Exercise; Produce the Product.

Select the Skill (Standard)

The particular skill or standard will need to initially address the student's grade-level expectation. Identify the task and cognitive complexity (see Defining Proficiency, pg.13) to determine which verbs and context are appropriate for that grade-level standard. More on how to approach the standard is detailed in Chapter 1, Standards-Based Grading.

Prepare the Concept

The *concept* is the key focus of understanding for any skill or standard. It is the concept we want students to internalize and interpret—not parrot back as memorized fact. The idea of a concept being learned is often presumed to be inherent in the teacher's instruction as much as it is presented in a student's completed assignment and, for many students, this may be the case. However, for those not inherently internalizing and interpreting the intended outcomes of instruction and assignments, there may be a need to address depths of understanding when it comes to preparing a concept for the purpose of intervention.

Let's look at a student in eighth grade that is struggling in math approximating the location of irrational numbers on a number line such as the square root of 2. What is the concept that the student is being expected to relay and how will we as teachers ask students to relay their understanding? For some teachers, there may not seem to be a concept needing to be relayed in the first place—knowing the location for the square root of 2 may not seem like a concept is being relayed. However, if you present the square root of 2 as a symbol for a particular value and equate it to any integer and its value to a particular positive or negative amount, you begin to see how the understanding of what the square root of 2 actually is as a concept can become the focus of an intervention session for a student or small group struggling with tasks related to this.

This example may require intervention that connects the understanding behind the square root of an irrational number with the square root of a rational number such as the square root of 4. It wouldn't be much to ask this student to draw a square and label each side length 2cm. Asking this student about this square's area should not be a stretch for this student and, if so, would provide insight into the grade-level standard this student may need to review or relearn (area is first introduced in third grade according to the *common core state standards*). If the student is able to explain the area as 4cm squared, then it may be possible to ask the student to connect this idea using rational numbers to the original question involving an irrational number. The trouble at this point will be how we ask a student to prove their understanding of this concept and, for this, it is important to consider the depths of understanding.

The idea of depths of understanding is first presented as six facets of understanding detailed in the 1998 book, *Understanding by Design*, written by Grant Wiggins and Jay McTighe. One of my own big takeaways from this book is the purposeful use (and also caution) of verbs and our understanding of words such as *understanding*. Students who claim they understand what was taught when they have only memorized what could be described as *knowledge* may be cause for concern from teachers if our intention is for students to have purposeful understanding of the content. With regard to the context of this chapter, what is most important is their *Six Facets of Understanding* and how we can use this idea to target our approach toward intervention.

SIX FACETS OF UNDERSTANDING					
1. Explain	2. Interpret	3. Apply	4. Perspective	5. Empathize	6. Self-Knowledge

SOURCE: Wiggins and McTighe (1998).

Teachers that utilize their curriculum resources for academic intervention will want to learn to adapt their resources to assess growth based on these six facets of understanding. The more facets with which a student is able to express a concept, the better their understanding is of that concept. When you apply this to a standards-based approach to intervention, assessing academic growth now has six means of identifying the depth of understanding. With each facet with which a student is able to communicate their understanding of a concept, the deeper their understanding of that concept is then supported with evidence.

Let's look again at that eighth-grade student working with square roots on a number line. In an intervention setting, this student may have shown extreme difficulty not only with this particular skill but also the prerequisite skills from prior grade levels that this grade-level expectation requires. When we begin to look at the depth of understanding required of this skill, we will begin to see how a student may have specific gaps that go back more than one academic year.

GRADE LEVEL	GRADE 6	GRADE 7	GRADE 8
Standard	Add and subtract integers and absolute value of integers. (6.NS.5,6,7)	Add and subtract absolute value of rational numbers using a number line. (7.NS.1)	Understand decimal expansion and convert into rational numbers including irrational approximations. (8.NS.1,2)
Example of Grade Level Standards			

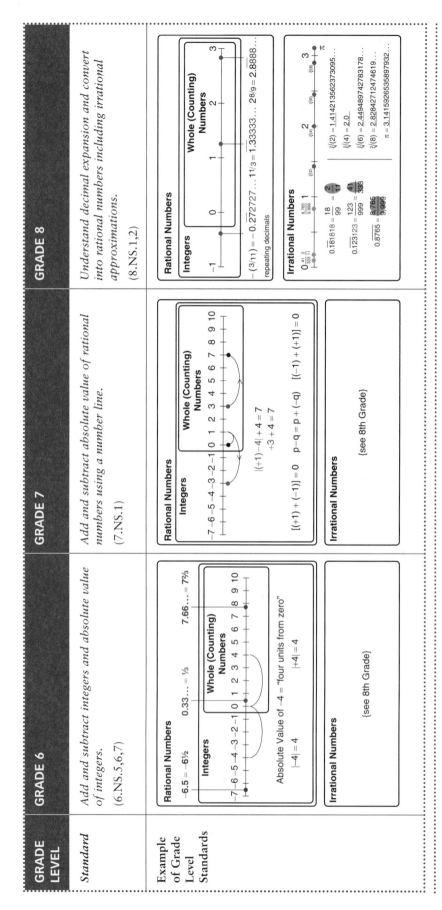

SOURCE: Images created with Exploring the Core Math 6-8 iOS/Android app.

The images included in the preceding progression of Grade 6–8 Number Sense standards are taken from the app *Exploring the Core: K–8 Math*. The app lets users swipe across grade-level skills to illustrate how skills in one grade level may have built on prior grade-level skills.

One example of how connecting the skills across grade levels is highlighted in the preceding images. In Grade 6, students are introduced to positive and negative integers on a number line and the concept of absolute value. This carries over to Grade 7 as students then apply Grade 6 knowledge of integers and strengthen their conceptual understanding of rational numbers on a number line. This becomes important as students in Grade 8 are then introduced to irrational numbers on a number line.

When we consider this skill development with regard to that same eighth-grade student from earlier in this chapter, it becomes clearer how grade-level expectations might require serious intervention that not only scaffolds related eighth-grade skills but connects the prior grade-level skills that may never have been learned.

It is also important to recognize in other more silent students who can draw a number line and memorize the location of a few rational and irrational numbers but miss the concept behind the skill. This limited understanding of irrational numbers will come back to haunt this student when irrational numbers appear in contexts other than a number line. Such gaps in learning specific to how standards develop across grade level is extremely important for teachers to not only understand for themselves but also communicate amongst themselves as a means of ongoing professional development. It will be necessary for the school's teachers to be transparent about the depth of understanding required for students to have mastered a particular skill. Those teachers that openly require only basic recall of a single facet of understanding in only one particular context will need to be transparent about this expectation so that teachers in later grade levels can prepare their instruction according to such depths of student understanding.

Develop the Tasks

Once the concept of a skill has been identified according to the standard being addressed, we will need to prepare tasks that provide students opportunities to explore a concept in ways that address at least one of the six facets of understanding. It may be tempting to request that students fulfill all six facets as proof of mastery but it may only be necessary (or even possible!) to provide evidence of understanding in two or three of these facets.

TASKS ACCORDING TO THE *SIX FACETS OF UNDERSTANDING*

Explain

Students may provide a verbal account of a concept, phenomena, that includes facts or data as support, or make insightful connections that provide illuminating examples.

Interpret

Students may provide an anecdote or translation of the concept, including a personal dimension to reflect meaningful context, or put the understanding through images, analogies, or models that are accessible according to their development.

Apply

Students may effectively use or adapt the concept in diverse and real contexts, to show they can *do* the subject through creation.

Perspective

Students may provide their own perspective of the concept through how they see and hear a different point of view through critical eyes and ears—are able to see the big picture.

Empathize

Students may express the value of a concept through contexts that others may find odd, alien, or implausible and sensitively perceive another's view on the basis of prior direct experience.

Self-Knowledge

Students may describe rationale, metacognitive awareness, perception of their own personal style, prejudices, projections, and habits of mind, that may both shape and impede understanding of the concept, in order to reflect on the meaning of learning experience in context of what may also be unknown based on what is known about the concept.

SOURCE: Understanding by Design (2nd Ed.), Wiggins and McTighe, 2005, pg. 84.

Developing the tasks that target understanding for the purpose of intervention will also need to incorporate the aspect of standards-based grading, defining proficiency. In this context, teachers will need to identify what is proficient for the student requiring intervention as much as it would be to identify the same for a student with an IEP. This may seem like an unequal comparison but, from the perspective of the teacher's role toward intervention, identifying what that student needs in order to adequately track progress toward meeting a specific intervention goal aligns with how teachers might read and apply an IEP in their classroom.

For this reason, I refer to Lee Ann Jung's 2018 book, *From Goals to Growth*, where she refers to a common challenge for teachers attempting to create measurement scales for academic growth. Defining proficiency for a student in an intervention setting may need to have a specific scale to measure growth toward meeting the academic goal (or goals) for the intervention. This may be as simple as breaking a particular skill into small measurable tasks with the intention of targeting a concept, but Jung recognizes that scaling tasks like this can feel overwhelming.

SKILL (STANDARD) *What are you learning?*	TASK *How will you practice?*	RESOURCE *What will you need to practice?*	STRATEGY *What steps will you take to practice?*	PRODUCT *What will show learning?*
3.NBT.1 *Rounding*	Q&A CHALLENGE	COUNTING CUBES, PENCIL/PAPER	ROUNDING POEM, NUMBER LINE	PRACTICE QUIZ, EXPLANATION

Scale for Practice/Product

Current Status (0) – Incorrect Solution, No Strategy

The student is not yet able to approach a rounding problem with an intentional strategy.

Level One (1) – Incorrect Solution, Strategy Attempted

The student recognizes rounding and recalls a strategy with no understanding of concept.

Level Two (2) – Correct Solution, Strategy Explained

The student approaches rounding using a strategy as a procedure for getting an answer.

Level Three (3) – Correct Solution, Multiple Strategies, Concept Applied

The student aptly describes how different strategies may be used to round numbers in a real-world word problem involving rounding (e.g., estimate a sum cost by rounding).

Level Four (4) – Correct Solution, Multiple Strategies and Facets of Understanding

The student is able to describe, interpret, apply contexts to demonstrate understanding of how the concept of rounding might benefit a particular situation.

The preceding example targets a third-grade math skill, rounding. By breaking up the skill into reasonably leveled expectations, growth can be measured over time with each practice session. The focus of this example is the *Scale for Practice/Product*. This example uses a four-point scale with each level defined by a clear expectation. Each level is also following Case's developmental steps allowing for the student to first assimilate a particular strategy in context of rounding (Level 1), apply a single strategy to solve a single problem (Level 2), extend this new learning to two strategies for a problem requiring two numbers to be rounded (Level 3), and finally elaborate on the learning to various facets of understanding (Level 4). It will be important to determine which level is the *goal* of the particular skill or standard for a given intervention session so the questions a teacher asks and tasks provided are appropriate to that expected level.

This may very well seem overwhelming for a teacher providing intervention for more than one student on any given day or week. Personally, I agree that it isn't only the process of creating a meaningful measurement scale that feels so overwhelming, it's creating from scratch a measurement scale for all skills that address multiple intervention students every few weeks. However, what I eventually came to realize is that students often have similar gaps in learning and that collecting the strategies and approaches for specific skills allows me to refer to prior intervention experiences to quickly adjust personalized measurement scales for students.

Jung also suggests to prevent or respond to this challenge, "acknowledge that this is a new approach and that the team will need to invest time and thought to develop a solid measurement scale. Even though it represents more work at the outset, team members will be paid back tenfold in how easy this process makes the subsequent tasks of progress monitoring and reporting" (p. 56). This is a very important insight to keep in mind as a student with gaps in their academic knowledge may require the teacher to identify and chunk the development of a skill into measurable tasks that can become a scale for measuring student growth through tasks in an intervention setting.

Practice: Prompt and Exercise

The strategies that a student uses in order to reach an academic goal will likely need to be provided (at least in part if not in full) by the teacher at first, prompted to use when appropriate, and exercised in various contexts. When the teacher selects the tasks appropriate for communicating the understanding of a concept, they will also need to provide various strategies that meet the needs of a student.

Observation of in-class student behaviors during instruction and practice may provide enough insight for a teacher to determine the most appropriate approach for a student. Whether this means the student would benefit more from physical manipulatives for building or constructing, instructional videos for pausing and multiple replays, a visual step-by-step cue card, one-on-one feedback discussion time, or some combination of strategies, it will be during this time that the student will be given positive affirmation of their potential through strategies the student can take with them for independent practice.

This is where the challenge becomes real for most students as they have likely been watching and listening to at least some classroom instruction on this concept. However, they may communicate their own misunderstanding of a particular part of the concept by saying, "I don't get it." This is where intervention not only provides the time to dig deep into what the student *does* understand about the concept in order to identify what they *do not* understand. This is where prompting can provide students the insight into what must be practiced in order to master a particular skill or concept.

It is important that the strategy be provided to the student as they leave the intervention session as a reminder of what they need to practice outside of the classroom. This does not need to be too terribly detailed—even a small memento to trigger their memory of the strategy may be all that is needed for the student to access the information when needed.

Produce the Product

It is one thing to have a student provide evidence of understanding during an intervention setting. It is a whole other thing to have a student come back a day or two after the intervention session where a concept was understood and have that student then provide evidence of understanding. It benefits the student to exercise their understanding of a concept through a task that requires more than a single intervention session to provide evidence of understanding—retention of student understanding also must be exercised.

When a student submits a product that exhibits one of the six facets of understanding, it will be up to the teacher to determine whether that student's work will serve as short-term knowledge or long-term understanding. It is for this reason that a student who is able to submit products that highlight more than one facet of understanding are more likely to retain their understanding of that concept. This may be done through multiple submissions much easier than it might be considered being done through a single task. One approach to providing students a framework for submitting tasks is the K – U – D approach:

- K - Knowledge
- U - Understand
- D - Do

The knowledge a student communicates after learning about a particular topic can serve as a basis for potential understanding of a concept. The concept behind the knowledge is where student understanding connects that knowledge to ideas beyond basic facts. These ideas may be expressed through statements of insight. It is these insightful statements that reflect understanding of a concept.

For example, that eighth-grade student from earlier in this chapter working with irrational numbers may have knowledge about exponents and square roots and recall that *two squared* equals *four* and that the *square root of four* equals *two*. However, asking that student to explain or interpret that knowledge in a way that is different than the equations written down may prove impossible without conceptual knowledge of square roots. Instead, imagine if the tasks this student submitted described an understanding of square roots such that the student could interpret square roots as the undoing of an exponent (or radical) for the purpose of identifying dimensions and amounts of perfect squares.

Consider the following example as *one* of many possible ways that an eighth-grade student can explain the concept behind square roots by drawing a square with side lengths of 2 units but describing each side as the *square root of four*. This student might now be better prepared to learn about square roots as they are applied to irrational numbers—for example, *the square root of forty-eight*.

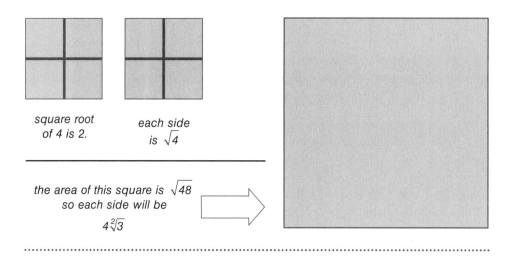

square root
of 4 is 2.

each side
is $\sqrt{4}$

the area of this square is $\sqrt{48}$
so each side will be
$4\sqrt[2]{3}$

$$\sqrt[2]{48} \qquad \sqrt[2]{3 \times 16} \qquad 4\sqrt[2]{3}$$

As that student begins to learn how square roots can be simplified, it is much more likely that they'll see the connection between rational square roots and their whole-number equivalents and the value of simplifying an irrational square root.

Once the student begins to recognize the connection between the square root of forty-eight and its approximate value of *four times the square root of three.*

The point of this eighth-grade example is to highlight the need for addressing the student's ability to explain the grade-level *concepts* in ways that make sense to them and are also mathematically accurate. This example also highlights the connection between the eighth-grade standard targeting irrational numbers and the prior grade-level standards targeting the understanding of rational numbers.

TIERS OF ACADEMIC INCLUSION

There are a variety of different ways that students may fall within or outside of the general academic expectations of a particular grade level. Some students may fall close enough to the academic expectations that in-class supports embedded in a curriculum guide are enough. However, it is common for the wide range of abilities in a classroom of students requires the adjustment of the classroom learning environment such that student academic needs are being met for all students.

I have experienced five tiers of students for which I have needed to adjust my classroom learning environment. I refer to these tiers when I prepare for a new school year:

1. **TAGs** – Talented and Gifted

2. **GenEds** – General Education

3. **RTIIs** – Response to Instruction and Intervention

4. **ELLs** – English Language Learner

5. **SpEds** – Special Education

The illustrations on the following page highlight the connection between how classrooms might view these tiers of academic inclusion as separate but included, compared to how classrooms can view these tiers as fully inclusive in the instructional plans.

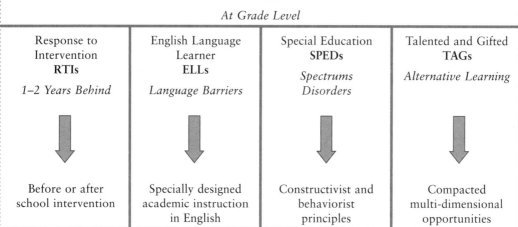

GENERAL ED MODEL: A general education model incorporates various learners "at grade level" into the design of the direct instruction of learning targets.

Gen Eds
At Grade Level

Response to Intervention **RTIs**	English Language Learner **ELLs**	Special Education **SPEDs**	Talented and Gifted **TAGs**
1–2 Years Behind	*Language Barriers*	*Spectrums Disorders*	*Alternative Learning*
Before or after school intervention	Specially designed academic instruction in English	Constructivist and behaviorist principles	Compacted multi-dimensional opportunities

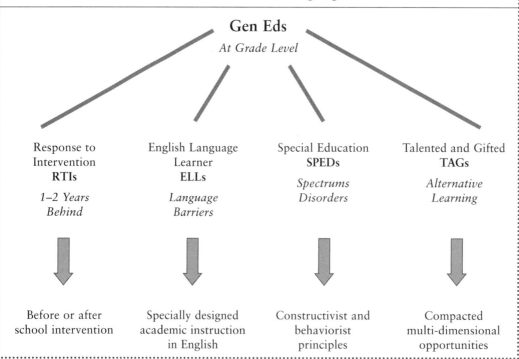

INCLUSION MODEL: An inclusion model incorporates all learners into the design of the direct instruction for each learning target.

Gen Eds
At Grade Level

Response to Intervention **RTIs**	English Language Learner **ELLs**	Special Education **SPEDs**	Talented and Gifted **TAGs**
1–2 Years Behind	*Language Barriers*	*Spectrums Disorders*	*Alternative Learning*
Before or after school intervention	Specially designed academic instruction in English	Constructivist and behaviorist principles	Compacted multi-dimensional opportunities

GenEds in my classroom are the broadest category of students and often include a mix of various student abilities that range within a year above or below in one content area or another. It is with this group that I target my backward-planning for the year and set my schedule for student academic expectations. GenEds will typically ebb and flow in out of my scheduled expectations throughout the year.

TAGs in my classroom are able to go beyond my instructional expectations in a majority of grade level standards but may not be placed officially in the next academic grade level for one reason or another. For these students, it is important to prepare ideas for compacting learning objectives that require students to go deeper into connecting multiple standards at once. These opportunities do not create a spotlight effect on their abilities in the classroom but still challenge those students in current grade-level standards. Compacted learning objectives also requires me to be more flexible with task timelines and deadlines or plan those activities to align with the rest of the class timelines and deadlines.

RTIIs in my classroom are typically GenEds that need specific support in various academic skills throughout the year. These students may have developed holes in their academic foundation by mastering enough standards in one grade level to move on to the next without addressing the prior year's academic deficiencies. If a student is receiving final reporting scores that show they continually master 70 to 90 percent of a grade level's standards, they may have been promoted through the grade levels without addressing that 10 to 30 percent of unlearned skills or related standards.

ELLs are typically provided a classroom environment that incorporates specially designed academic instruction in English (SDAIE) resources and strategies that target multi-sensory supports for background information of individual skills and related standards. This may overlap with RTIIs with added visual and oral scaffolding for those that may not have the English language support at home or in their community.

SpEds might require any number of specific supports. These identifications are typically provided in writing and include specific classroom accommodations or content modifications. I appreciate having these requirements spelled out for me ahead of time, so I can prepare my classroom and lessons accordingly. The way I approach SpEds in my inclusive model is to determine the range of needs required in my classroom and overlap those needs to match with the ELLs, RTIIs, GenEds, and TAGs in my classroom. This way, I am able to identify which supports are already being provided in my classroom that overlap with the accommodations of my SpEds, and which accommodations for my SpEds may be beneficial to the majority of students in my classroom.

TIERS OF DEVELOPMENTAL INCLUSION

My most recent experience has been in including nonacademic development into my standards-based instructional approach. In this section, I will describe my experience with the blending of cognitive and psychosocial developmental concepts into my instructional approach.

Cognitive Tiers (Piaget's Cognitive Stages of Development)

These cognitive tiers are organized by age ranges and therefore, at least in the United States, can be organized by grade level ranges. However, the degree of overlap between tiers is not subject to any specific limit of age or grade level.

- **Preoperational:** Ages 2 to 7 (Grades PreK to 2).
- **Concrete Operational:** Ages 7 to 11 (Grades 2 to 6).
- **Formal Operational:** Ages 11 to Adult (Grades 6–12+).

Psychosocial Tiers (Erikson's Psychosocial Stages of Development)

These psychosocial tiers are organized by age ranges and therefore by grade-level ranges. However, the degree of overlap between tiers is not subject to any specific age or grade level.

- **Initiative versus Guilt:** Ages 3 to 5 (Grades PreK to Kindergarten).
- **Industry versus Inferiority:** Ages 5 to 13 (Grades Kindergarten to Grade 8).
- **Identify versus Role Confusion:** Ages 13 to 21 (Grades 8 to 12+).

It is important to note that these developmental tiers can blend both academic and behavioral components into this academic inclusion approach. This is because of the fluidity that occurs in social-emotional learning and the similar nature of cognitive and psychosocial development does play a role in academic development, but I will do my best to address only the overlap of standards-based academic learning with cognitive and psychosocial development.

Developmental tiers are not subgroups and are not subject to strict hardlines of age-based development. Cognitive and psychosocial development work in tandem in all humans and it is important to note that these ages are not hard lines. It is also important to note that stages do not end in their development but evolve in complexity to support an increase in student capacity for learning.

As both sets of stages develop over time, recognize that an individual student will experience different rates of development for both sets of stages. The transitions themselves between both sets of developmental stages must also be considered. Because these transitions are not hard lines, two stages may appear to be developing at the same time. Since I am only able to observe these stages of development through student behavior, for example, I could have a student who needs a concrete explanation of one specific abstract idea, but still be able to explain another abstract idea with only hypothetical discussion and reasoning.

As I discuss developmental tiers and consider the overlapping nature of each set of stages, as a teacher, I must remember one thing: while instruction guides development, development must also guide instruction. This means that I will not be able to include in my lesson plans which developmental tier I am addressing in order to teach a specific standard. Instead, I must use my awareness of these developmental tiers to adjust my instruction as I observe students struggling with specific lessons. In this way, my awareness of developmental tiers adds to a learning environment of academic inclusion that can incorporate all students.

Note: Because time is a limited classroom resource, teachers will feel overwhelmed at the idea of addressing all student concerns for every lesson taught. However, as I combine this developmental perspective toward both academic inclusion and behavioral coaching of SEL components, I am increasing the effectiveness of the Self-Directed Learning environment.

ACADEMIC INTERVENTION

In my experience, the phrase *academic intervention* is commonly used to describe services to students unable to meet grade-level academic expectations. Grade-level standards are the chief academic expectations and any student unable to meet a relatively proficient mastery of those standards will require academic intervention. Efforts to provide scaffolding or other academic support in an intervention setting must be in response to instructional strategies taking place in the classroom. This means that classroom instructional strategies must be observed and recorded with the intent and purpose of providing academic intervention as needed.

Intervention in the Classroom

Not all intervention strategies are effective for all students in all classrooms.

To say there are common classroom instructional strategies that are best suited for academic intervention in the classroom is to refer too broadly to a wide collection of individual strategies. Many teachers, schools, districts, professors, nonprofits, research facilities, and publishing companies may refer to a variety of effective classroom instructional strategies. To list all effective and noneffective strategies from across the country would result in an encyclopedia of resources and strategies that, by itself, would serve little purpose besides being a reference for those seeking a specific strategy or resource. It is for this reason that I believe any one strategy, approach, or resource is not necessarily going to be the best suited for all teachers and all students in all schools.

Whichever instructional strategy a teacher implements, the value of the intervention strategy will be most influenced by how student learning is tracked in the classroom. This requires an approach that organizes expected academic skills in such a way that a teacher can communicate exactly what skills have been learned over time and to what depth of proficiency those skills have been learned. Standards-Based Learning is the approach that I prefer to use because it breaks down all skills into standards that can be easily tracked according to proficiency expectations embedded into each standard.

Before introducing any standard, it may help to spend time teaching the related standards from prior grade levels. This gives immediate feedback on which students will need small group attention and which students may only need this review to recall or relearn content forgotten or not fully understood in a prior grade level. By applying this form of preventative intervention within my general instruction model, I avoid having to give students a *test* that may be subjective or limiting in what each student relates to or remembers about a specific skill or topic.

During instruction of a standard, students struggling with a skill are not immediately placed into an intervention setting. I typically use a small group setting with a variety of different student configurations over several days to discuss the skill in different contexts. This allows various students from their varied background of knowledge and ability to explain a skill or topic in a way that may connect with a student struggling with the idea. It is important that I am there for this conversation so that I may correct any misconceptions or miscommunications.

At this point, it would be reasonable to do a one-on-one session with students to determine whether it is needed to address a foundation skill from a prior grade level and connect it to the current grade-level standard.

It is likely that more than one student may have missed that skill and might find themselves interested in the in-class intervention being provided. The focus on developing cognitive complexity by targeting related skills from prior grade levels may spark an initial interest in students as it may highlight positive affirmation of their knowledge from past learning.

During this process of in-class intervention, the concept of a self-directed learning environment supports the idea that the rest of the students are targeting skills through tasks they've determined not only meet their interests but also meet expectations for mastery of their grade-levels standards.

Intervention Out of the Classroom

Each year, I continue to adjust and adapt to the needs of different students. I find myself including an increasing number of intervention-style strategies to in-class academic instructional approach as I continue to find more ways to address specific student needs within the classroom. However, there are students who require targeted intervention to support those foundational skills or standards outside of the classroom in focused small group or individualized intervention settings.

I typically work with students in an intervention setting outside of the classroom for a short time afterschool—with permission from the parent or guardian. For older students, it can be before school, during a prep period, or after school based on schedule and availability. When I have only a few students requiring intervention, each session can be very productive for all students. When too many students are involved in a single intervention session, the quality of that intervention declines as it becomes more like a regular classroom setting. I find the best value for intervention is with one to five students per session. This allows for all questions to be asked in an environment where students can still engage and help each other.

It benefits the students, their parents, and administration to know in which skills or standards students are needing intervention. Again, this is where a standards-based approach is beneficial. Objectively target specific standards needing to be mastered and the intervention sessions can be scheduled accordingly. This also helps to determine when intervention is no longer needed for specific students. When documenting students requiring intervention, it may seem like a lot of paperwork to identify and track progress of specific skills based on evidence collected from the student. However, intervention cannot only serve to promote academic growth but also to strengthen goal-setting and self-reflection capacity of individual students.

If a student is unsure as to why they are attending intervention outside of the classroom, either they are being told to attend intervention without understanding its purpose, or they are embarrassed about being in an intervention setting and afraid to admit to themselves that they need help—they may also have simply forgotten. I like to provide students a standards-based proficiency tracker that allows them to quickly refer to what standards they have or have not mastered. The style and formatting of this tracker can be designed to appropriately match the age of the student. If students are still working on responsibility and organization of belongings, I may keep these trackers in my classroom.

STANDARDS-BASED PROFICIENCY TRACKER—EXAMPLE

Standard: RL.3.2   **Topic:** Main Idea & Key Details.

Recount stories, including fables, folktales, and myths from diverse cultures; determine the central message, lesson, or moral and explain how it is conveyed through key details in the text.

Proficient Level: 1   2   3   4

Level 1 Proficient   Recall/Reproduction

I can . . . identify the main idea of a story from a list of possible answers.

Evidence, Date

Story and quiz, 9/5	

Level 2 Proficient   Communicate Concept/Skill

I can . . . describe the main idea of a story appropriate for Grade 3.

Evidence, Date

Story and sentence, 9/15	
Story and sentence, 9/20	

Level 3 Proficient   Evidence-Based Strategic Thinking & Reasoning

I can . . . explain the main idea of a story with supporting details.

Evidence, Date

Story and paragraph, 9/29	
Story and paragraph, 10/4	
Story and paragraph, 10/11	

Level 4 Proficient   Extended Thinking Beyond Instructional Materials

I can . . . connect the main idea of two stories referring to specific details that support the similarities of both stories.

Evidence, Date

Story and quiz, 10/18	

Knowing which skills or standards are needing to be addressed, a teacher is better able to provide resources and strategies that target those individual student needs. Some intervention sessions may target a skill or standard common among the students while other sessions will be independent or involve partner rotations where the teacher can work more closely with a few students at a time. The benefit of limiting the overall time of the intervention sessions is that the teacher can target a very specific skill and strategy, provide positive feedback, and have each student leave the intervention session with a small task that is well within their reach to complete.

Intervention sessions also provide opportunities for students to ask me the questions they may not have been comfortable asking in the classroom. For these students, this also allows teachers to connect with and guide these few students in mirroring strategies for building self-efficacy in the classroom. It also provides opportunities for students to be reassured that, even when the teacher will be instructing the next level of a skill in the classroom, these students know they are closing the gaps needed to eventually reach the grade-level standards. Especially when these students work on specific intervention skills and strategies and connect them to what is happening in the classroom, it is these social-emotional components of self-efficacy and improvement as well as self-reflection and goal-setting that make these intervention sessions so important to the effectiveness of intervention out of the classroom.

Conclusion

ADOPT AND ADAPT

As I close this book, I want to express one final time my desire that each concept in my framework be adopted and adapted to meet the needs of any individual community, campus, administration, classroom, teacher, parent, and student. Adopting without regard for the needs being met through the adoption of a framework or program results in a variety of reactions from all involved in the process of student learning. The adapting of my framework is what allows for each concept to utilize existing programs within a school's vision to make ongoing and long-lasting changes to a school's climate.

Adapting any one concept in my framework is similar to any new learning from a cognitive standpoint. It begins with assimilating an idea through language to instill a concept. As the concept begins to take shape in the eyes of a staff or class, questions then arise as procedures begin to address specific individual factors and concerns. At that point, discussion can evolve to consider coordinating two factors of a concept as each person involved finds ways for their own learning environment to coordinate and utilize multiple factors of a single concept. What is most important to consider is the idea that changing the vision of an educational institution is extremely difficult and should take time to ensure that healthy shifts in philosophy move together.

I like the analogy of steering a fleet of ships and how ships in front leading the rest will impact how a fleet changes course. The major difference in this analogy is that the military has a specific culture of following orders that may be stricter in that setting than it might be in a particular school.

It may be common for a school's administration to lead from the front and expect all teachers to follow orders and turn alongside them. It may also be common for a school's administration to position a few lead teachers amongst the staff and brief them on changes that will take place in order to assist in a planned school-wide adjustment in direction. These common approaches represent an approach that administration may support and implement from the top, down to all staff. However, when it comes to the concepts discussed in this book, be wary that this can result in high turnover of teachers that are unwilling to adapt to what an administration may be excited to adopt.

Instead, it is recommended that top-down support of a bottom-up approach is considered.

> In a bottom-up approach, teachers develop the progressions based on their experience and work 'collaboratively to identify the sub skills or sub concepts that would lead to understanding of the concept or acquisition of the skill. (Heritage, 2008, p. 17)

> We posit that this bottom-up approach with top-down support is the most conducive to developing rigorous, developmentally appropriate competencies and learning progressions that teachers base on other teachers' and their own input and recognized expertise. This also provides teachers with the leeway to refine the competencies and progressions as necessary, truly allowing them to evolve organically. (Stack & Vander Els, 2018, p. 55)

Adopting an entire framework can be inherently overwhelming and I recognize the need for any educational institution to tread lightly when approaching a framework that may result in an adjusted vision toward student learning. In the following paragraphs, it will be suggested that each primary concept be adopted such that a school's teachers can adapt to the changes organically. When deciding which concept to begin, my recommendation is with the academics targeting a Standards-Based Grading. In my experience, students are quick to adopt and adapt standards-based grading practices when their teachers provide adequate support and rationale. It is not for the students but for the sake of administrators, teachers, and parents that the concepts of this framework and philosophy be seen as a change in perspective toward student learning, to be introduced and developed as any new learning would be—tracking growth (of new ideas) toward proficiency (of each concept) over time.

For those looking to adopt this framework and philosophy, my suggested path for adapting each concept would be to start with Standards-Based Learning as a concept. Do this for a year. Shift the perspective of learning toward isolated academic evidence and growth. Once this first concept begins to evolve in classrooms, behavior and a student's self-efficacy and responsibility become a separate issue, homework and participation grading practices shift, and objective measures for student growth begin to take hold. This is due to the necessary separation of behavioral reporting from academic reporting involved in standards-based learning.

While standards-based learning continues to evolve in classrooms, aspects of student behavior then become the focus as students begin to recognize their ability to track their own progress with objective goals, support their peers with transparent grading practices, and develop the shift in perspective that builds on a community of learning rather than individual success. This is where the second concept can be adapted to meet both the social and the emotional needs for a particular community of students. As the components of social-emotional learning become internalized by a school's staff, a common language can be assimilated into everyday school procedures. It is this shift in perspective by a school's staff that is responsible for a school's culture to begin changing. Students notice this change and, while a percentage of students may challenge a changing culture out of sheer resilience against changing their own perspectives and beliefs about school, most students will naturally conform to this ongoing shift in cohesive perspective and academic leadership.

As standards-based grading and social-emotional learning begin to be adapted in classrooms across a school campus, students begin recognizing their value as learners and can be coached to track their own academic progress in a standards-based learning environment. This is what creates over time a *Self-Directed Learning* environment where specific tools can be provided for students as they learn to master each academic skill in their grade level at their own pace. For many students, they are quick to realize how other students (even those that they hadn't considered friends before) can become valuable resources and begin to balance the enjoyment they have with other students with the learning that occurs.

At this point, the theories of human development, cognitively and psychosocially, will likely become observable conversations as the self-directed learning environment develops. This allows a wider range of accommodations to be adapted to meet the needs of each student and support the contemporary adage: "all means each." As teachers begin to provide students with the resources and guidance beyond knowing *what* to learn but knowing *how* to learn, recognizing academic and behavior challenges with a developmental mindset allows the patience needed to identify solutions to meet individual student needs. For example, some students who did not develop executive functioning skills at earlier ages will need more structural oversight. Other students who did not receive opportunities to develop concrete operational reasoning in one area or another may need more hands-on concrete academic tasks. There may also be students who are transitioning early into a psychosocial stage of *identity versus role confusion* that may set themselves apart from their peers or cause unnecessary confusion or strife among their peers out of response to this development. These examples are snapshots of a seemingly infinite amount of considerations when addressing a fully inclusive self-directed learning environment.

Behavioral coaching and intervention is a natural next step for a fully inclusive self-directed learning environment. Gaps in academic learning that are found to be directly influenced by environmental, social, or cultural factors can then be addressed separate from the academic learning. Self-management and efficacy, goal-setting, empathy, interpersonal skills, conflict resolution—these are all areas that an individual student may also have gaps that are impeding academic growth. Spending time connecting with these individual or small groups of students and providing strategies in a discussion setting might have a wide range of impacts on student learning. Designing behavioral intervention for a classroom or a school will take insight into the specific challenges needing to be addressed and an appropriate response given available resources (time, staffing, etc.). Comprehensive *out-of-the-box* programs may meet many classroom or school needs but will still need to be adapted at all levels of its implementation to ensure students receive only the most imperative resources and guidance.

It is at this point that teachers may have the data and developmental mindset to provide strategic academic intervention to support the self-directed learning environment being cultivated. Recognizing students who may be learning at a slower rate than their peers may be due to particular gaps in specific skill development. A student who may have previously received in a traditional grading system B's and C's likely missed 10 to 30 percent of the material they needed to have mastered, and it is now those gaps in learning that are causing more complex skill sets to be more difficult than necessary. Identifying those gaps takes time. Specific intervention may be necessary for small groups or individual students. Behavior must be separated from academic need when addressing academic intervention to avoid conflating academic gaps in learning from an unwillingness to meet general behavioral expectations.

When it comes to intervention, both academically and behaviorally, it is important to recognize the impact a resource or guidance may have on an individual student's development, cognitively or psychosocially. Although it cannot be guaranteed that a student will or will not be ready for a specific strategy or approach, recognizing where a student is in their development can help narrow the most appropriate strategies and approaches. A younger student may not be ready for discussions where hypothetical reasoning is the approach—imaginative play that targets reflection toward other students' feelings and acting out behaviors that garner peer support and reciprocation may be the best approach for students at these younger stages of development. However, students who have spent years developing through a concrete operational stage of reasoning and showing interest in somewhat hypothetical situations, such as the *gray areas* of human behavior and the judicious use of a school's rules, punishments, or rewards, may need more strategic discussion sessions each week that provide them opportunities to organize these thoughts into an organized framework that makes sense to them.

As concepts of standards-based learning, social-emotional learning, and human development begin to overlap over time, a whole-child approach will begin to emerge, while each classroom aligns with one vision that will slowly change the climate of the school to meet the needs of a community's students and staff. The result will hopefully provide a means of purposeful exploration into the core of creating a self-directed learning environment that helps redefine why we are at school together, developing skills and knowledge over time, becoming well-balanced members of larger communities.

QUOTES TO CONSIDER

There were many quotes intended to be included within the content of this book. I decided to include them in this unique section to focus the content of each chapter on the larger framework and philosophy. There are many authors writing on the very concepts presented in this book. I hope readers of this book find joy in exploring these ideas further in an effort to connect and adapt these concepts within a single approach that helps meet the needs of your community's students. Accept the following quotes as thoughts to consider in an effort to spur your own exploration of what I personally see as the core of human learning.

Standards-Based Grading

Teachers should emphasize more recent information when it provides a more accurate picture of student achievement, and students should be given second (or more) chances to demonstrate what they know, understand, and can do on varied methods of assessment. It means that final grades should virtually never be determined by simply averaging the grades from several grading periods (e.g., adding the grades from Terms 1 through 3 and then dividing by 3) . . . teachers need to keep their records—on paper or on a computer—in ways that can easily be changed or updated. "Grade in pencil" may not always be literal advice, but it needs to be the mind-set that teachers have about recording grades. (O'Connor, 2009, p. 149)

The components of a target-based assessment, grading, and reporting system can be broken into four concepts: de-emphasizing grading formative practice, allowing for reassessment to occur on summative assessments, grading behaviors and life skills separate from academic grades, and assigning academic grades based on student proficiency against specific learning targets. (Hierck & Larson, 2018, p. 14)

Social-Emotional Learning

Whether or not there is a class explicitly devoted to emotional literacy may matter far less than how these lessons are taught. There is perhaps no subject where the quality of the teacher matters so much, since how a teacher handles her class is in itself a model, a de facto lesson in emotional competence—or the lack thereof. Whenever a teacher responds to one student, twenty or thirty others learn a lesson. (Goleman, 1995, p. 279)

Teachers who recognize that social and emotional health and growth are critical to learning carefully work with children's outbursts or unacceptable behavior. They know that their modeling is critical to how children will react toward others. They know that children can learn social-emotional skills that will enhance the quality of learning. Finally, they believe that children can resolve conflict and become responsible decision makers and problem solvers. (Elias & Arnold, 2006, p. 69)

Cognitive strain is affected by both the current level of effort and the presence of unmet demands . . . a sentence that is printed in a clear font, or has been repeated, or has been primed, will be fluently processed with cognitive ease. Hearing a speaker when you are in a good mood, or even when you have a pencil stuck crosswise in your mouth to make you 'smile' also induces cognitive ease. (Kahneman, 2011, p. 59)

The predictive value of three aspects of teacher beliefs regarding teachers' promotion of self-regulated learning (SRL) is modelled by means of structural equation modelling. These include teacher beliefs on (1) instructing SRL, (2) regarding their own self-efficacy towards the promotion of SRL, and (3) their epistemological beliefs regarding learning. (Dignath-van Ewijk, 2016, pp. 83–105)

Self-Directed Learning

It may seem counterintuitive to place more control of learning in the hands of [low-achieving students]. The tendency may be, rather, to assign them more individual seatwork—to give them lower-level work that they can handle. But already-frustrated students and tedium do not mix well. (Rollins, 2014, p. 95)

Few of us are prepared to accept that it is our attempts to control that destroys the only thing we have with our children that gives us some control over them, our relationship. (Glasser, 1998, p. 196)

Another important aspect of thinking for oneself is making decisions and solving problems. When we are told and controlled, we have few decisions to make or problems to solve. Yet life is a steady stream of decisions and crises . . . To learn to make decisions, we first need decisions to make. SDL provides them. (Gibbons, 2002, p. 61)

But if we are truly going to prepare them for life outside of school, then we need to teach them how to access and understand content on their own, not package it in a lecture of a PowerPoint and present it to them. This is the first step in changing instruction, switching from input delivery . . . to input discovery. The problem? The first is so much easier and so much more predictable. (Rinkema & Williams, 2018, p. 91)

Improvements to self-regulation during childhood lead to better adult outcomes (Moffitt et al., 2011). This research suggests that when we show children like Jon how to intentionally regulate their thoughts, emotions, and behavior, we can empower them to live a life in which they can act in accordance with their intentions, pursuing the goals and upholding the standards that are important to them. (Yeager & Yeager, 2013, p. 17)

Sources of Motivation (Resources and Citations)

Battistone, W., Buckmiller, T., & Peters, R. (2019). Assessing assessment literacy: Are new teachers prepared to assume jobs in school districts engaging in grading and assessment reform efforts? *Studies in Educational Evaluation, 62,* 10–17.

Biggs, J. (1999). What the student does: Teaching for enhanced learning. *Higher Education Research & Development, 18*(1), 57–75.

Brabrand, C. (2008). Constructive alignment for teaching model-based design for concurrency. In *Transactions on petri nets and other models of concurrency I* (pp. 1–18). Springer, Berlin, Heidelberg.

Case, R. (1991). *The mind's staircase: Exploring the conceptual underpinnings of children's thought and knowledge.* New York: Psychology Press.

Chappuis, S., Commodore, C., & Stiggins, R. (2016). *Balanced assessment systems: Leadership, quality, and the role of classroom assessment.* Thousand Oaks, CA: Corwin.

Chiu, C. L. (2017). Keep them engaged! Using self-monitoring checklists to increase assignment completion. *The Journal of the Effective Schools Project, 24*(24).

Cristóvão, A. M., Candeias, A. A., & Verdasca, J. (2017). Social and emotional learning and academic achievement in Portuguese schools: A bibliometric study. *Frontiers in Psychology, 8,* 1913.

Dawkins, R. (2016). *The selfish gene.* Oxford, UK: Oxford University Press.

Dignath-van Ewijk, C. (2016). Which components of teacher competence determine whether teachers enhance self-regulated learning? Predicting teachers' self-reported promotion of self-regulated learning by means of teacher beliefs, knowledge, and self-efficacy. *Frontline Learning Research, 4*(5), 83–105.

Doucleff, M. (2019). Teaching kids to control their anger. https://www.npr.org/2019/03/10/701987119/teaching-kids-to-control-their-anger

Einhorn, H. J., & Hogarth, R. M. (1981). Behavioral decision theory: Processes of judgement and choice. *Annual Review of Psychology, 32*(1), 53–88.

Elias, M. J., & Arnold, H. (2006). *The educator's guide to emotional intelligence and academic achievement: Social-emotional learning in the classroom.* Thousand Oaks, CA: Corwin.

Emberson, L. L., Cannon, G., Palmeri, H., Richards, J. E., & Aslin, R. N. (2017). Using fNIRS to examine occipital and temporal responses to stimulus repetition in young infants: Evidence of selective frontal cortex involvement. *Developmental Cognitive Neuroscience, 23*, 26–38.

Erikson, E. H. (1966). Eight ages of man. *International Journal of Psychiatry, 2*(3), 281–300.

Francis, A., & Flanigan, A. (2012). Self-directed learning and higher education practices: Implications for student performance and engagement. *MountainRise, 7*(3).

Fullan, M. (2012). *Change forces: Probing the depths of educational reform.* London: Routledge.

Galla, B. M., Plummer, B. D., White, R. E., Meketon, D., D'Mello, S. K., & Duckworth, A. L. (2014). The Academic Diligence Task (ADT): Assessing individual differences in effort on tedious but important schoolwork. *Contemporary Educational Psychology, 39*(4), 314–325.

Gaustad, J. (1994). Nongraded education: Overcoming obstacles to implementing the multiage classroom. Special Issue. *OSSC Bulletin, 38*, n3–4.

Gibbons, M. (2002). *The self-directed learning handbook: Challenging adolescent students to excel.* San Francisco: John Wiley & Sons.

Glasser, W. (1998). *The choice theory: A new psychology of personal freedom* (Kim, IJ & Woo, AR Trans). Seoul, Korea: Counseling center.

Goleman, D. (1995). *Emotional intelligence.* New York: Bantam Books.

Guide, C. A. S. E. L. (2013). *Effective social and emotional learning programs.* Preschool and Elementary School Edition (9/12).

Hansson, S. O. (1994). *Decision theory—A brief introduction.* Stockholm, Sweden: Department of Philosophy and the History of Technology, Royal Institute of Technology (KTH).

Heritage, M. (2008). *Learning progressions: Supporting instruction and formative assessment.* Washington, DC: Council of Chief State School Officers.

Hess, K. (2018). *A local assessment toolkit to promote deeper learning: Transforming research into practice.* Thousand Oaks, CA: Corwin.

Hierck, T., & Larson, G. (2018). *Grading for impact: Raising student achievement through a target-based assessment and learning system.* Thousand Oaks, CA: Corwin.

Immordino-Yang, M. H., & Damasio, A. (2007). We feel, therefore we learn: The relevance of affective and social neuroscience to education. *Mind, Brain, and Education, 1*(1), 3–10.

Jung, L. A. (2018). *From goals to growth: Intervention & support in every classroom.* Alexandria, VA: ASCD.

Kahneman, D. (2011). *Thinking, fast and slow.* Toronto: Anchor Canada.

Kleiman, M. (2009). *When brute force fails: How to have less crime and less punishment.* Princeton: Princeton University Press.

Kohn, A. (2016). *The myth of the spoiled child: Coddled kids, helicopter parents, and other phony crises.* Boston, MA: Beacon Press.

Lawson, G. M., McKenzie, M. E., Becker, K. D., Selby, L., & Hoover, S. A. (2018). The core components of evidence-based social emotional learning programs. *Prevention Science, 20*, 1–11.

Mantz, L. S. (2017). School-based social-emotional development: The role of relationships and teaching (Doctoral dissertation, University of Delaware). *The Manual of Child Development.* (1955). New York: University Society.

McCarty, K. (2006). *Full inclusion: The benefits and disadvantages of inclusive schooling. An overview.* Online Submission.

Miller, S. A. (2017). *Developmental research methods.* Englewood Cliffs, NJ: Prentice-Hall.

Moffitt, T. E., Arseneault, L., Belsky, D., Dickson, N., Hancox, R. J., Harrington, H., . . . & Sears, M. R. (2011). A gradient of childhood self-control predicts health, wealth, and public safety. *Proceedings of the National Academy of Sciences, 108*(7), 2693–2698.

Nakagawa, T. (2017, September). *'Liberty vs. Love': The principal contradiction of human culture (2) The 'Liberty vs. Love' contradiction and 'Ethics' at the personal level.* In Japan Creativity Society Annual Conference.

Neff, K. D. (2003). The development and validation of a scale to measure self-compassion. *Self and Identity, 2*(3), 223–250.

Neff, K. D., Hsieh, Y. P., & Dejitterat, K. (2005). Self-compassion, achievement goals, and coping with academic failure. *Self and Identity, 4*(3), 263–287.

Niebling, B. C. (2012). Determining the cognitive complexity of the Iowa Core in literacy and mathematics: Implications and applications for curriculum alignment. Des Moines: Iowa Department of Education.

O'Connor, K. (Ed.). (2009). *How to grade for learning, K–12.* Thousand Oaks, CA: Corwin.

Perry, B. D. (2006). Applying principles of neurodevelopment to clinical work with maltreated and traumatized children: The neurosequential model of therapeutics. In N. B. Webb (Ed.), *Working with traumatized youth in child welfare* (pp. 27–52). New York: Guilford Press.

Petit, M., & Hess, K. (2006). Applying Webb's Depth-of-Knowledge (DOK) and NAEP levels of complexity in mathematics. Dover NH: National Center for Assessment. https://www.rcoe.us/educational-services/files/2013/08/DOK-Math.pdf

Piaget, J. (1928). *Judgment and reasoning in the child.* Oxford, England: Harcourt, Brace. http://dx.doi.org/10.4324/9780203207260

Plutchik, R. (2001). The nature of emotions: Human emotions have deep evolutionary roots, a fact that may explain their complexity and provide tools for clinical practice. *American Scientist, 89*(4), 344–350.

Price, G. R., Yeo, D. J., Wilkey, E. D., & Cutting, L. E. (2018). Prospective relations between resting-state connectivity of parietal subdivisions and arithmetic competence. *Developmental Cognitive Neuroscience, 30*, 280–290.

Rinkema, E., & Williams, S. (2018). *The standards-based classroom: Make learning the goal.* Thousand Oaks, CA: Corwin.

Rodriguez, M. C., Dosedel, M., & Kang, Y. (2019, April). Interpretation and use validation of social and emotional learning measures in inequitable settings. Paper presented at the annual meeting of the American Educational Research Association, Toronto, Canada. https://sites.google.com/view/mnydrg/research

Roeser, R. W., Eccles, J. S., & Sameroff, A. J. (2000). School as a context of early adolescents' academic and social-emotional development: A summary of research findings. *The Elementary School Journal, 100*(5), 443–471.

Rollins, S. P. (2014). *Learning in the fast lane: 8 ways to put ALL students on the road to academic success.* Alexandria, VA: ASCD.

Shaw, S. C. K. (2017). How can we promote and facilitate effective study skills in medical students? *MedEdPublish, 6*(1).

Simms, J. A. (2017). *Critical concepts: Alignment to source standards.* Marzano Research.

Stack, B. M., & Vander Els, J. G. (2018). *Breaking with tradition: The shift to competency-based learning in PLCs at work.* Bloomington, IN: Solution Tree Press.

Tan, L., & Koh, J. H. (2014). *Self-directed learning: Learning in the 21st century.* Singapore: Educational Technology Division, Ministry of Education.

Tanenhaus, M. K., Flanigan, H. P., & Seidenberg, M. S. (1980). Orthographic and phonological activation in auditory and visual word recognition. *Memory & Cognition, 8*(6), 513–520.

Tomlinson, C. A. (2014). *The differentiated classroom: Responding to the needs of all learners.* Moorabbin, Victoria: Hawker Brownlow Education.

Vedantam, S. (2017, March 13). Hidden Brain, Episode 64, "I'm Right, You're Wrong."

Vogel-Scibilia, S. E., McNulty, K. C., Baxter, B., Miller, S., Dine, M., & Frese, F. J. (2009). The recovery process utilizing Erikson's stages of human development. *Community Mental Health Journal, 45*(6), 405.

Watts, T. W., Duncan, G. J., & Quan, H. (2018). Revisiting the marshmallow test: A conceptual replication investigating links between early delay of gratification and later outcomes. *Psychological Science, 29*(7), 1159–1177.

Webb, N. L., Alt, M., Ely, R., & Vesperman, B. (2005). Web alignment tool. Wisconsin Center of Educational Research. University of Wisconsin-Madison.

Wiggins, G., & McTighe, J. (1998). *Understanding by Design.* Alexandria, VA: Merrill Education/ASCD.

Wylie, C., & Lyon, C. (2013). Using the formative assessment rubrics, reflection and observation tools to support professional reflection on practice. *Pridobljeno, 5,* 2018.

Yeager, D. S., Henderson, M. D., Paunesku, D., Walton, G. M., D'Mello, S., Spitzer, B. J., & Duckworth, A. L. (2014). Boring but important: A self-transcendent purpose for learning fosters academic self-regulation. *Journal of Personality and Social Psychology, 107*(4), 559.

Yeager, M., & Yeager, D. (2013). *Executive function & child development.* New York: WW Norton & Company.

Yildirim, I., Akan, D., & Yalçin, S. (2016). Teacher behavior unwanted according to student's perceptions. *International Education Studies, 9*(11), 1–12.

Yousaf, A., & Khan, T. (2014). Recognition of cognitive development stages in students with reference to Pagetian cognitive stages. *International Journal of English and Education, 3*(2), 410–422.

Zins, J. E., Bloodworth, M. R., Weissberg, R. P., & Walberg, H. J. (2007). The scientific base linking social and emotional learning to school success. *Journal of Educational and Psychological Consultation, 17*(2–3), 191–210.

Index

CORWIN A SAGE Publishing Company

CORWIN HAS ONE MISSION: to enhance education through intentional professional learning.

We build long-term relationships with our authors, educators, clients, and associations who partner with us to develop and continuously improve the best evidence-based practices that establish and support lifelong learning.

Solutions YOU WANT | Experts YOU TRUST | Results YOU NEED

EVENTS >>> **INSTITUTES**

Corwin Institutes provide large regional events where educators collaborate with peers and learn from industry experts. Prepare to be recharged and motivated!

corwin.com/institutes

ON-SITE PD >>> **ON-SITE PROFESSIONAL LEARNING**

Corwin on-site PD is delivered through high-energy keynotes, practical workshops, and custom coaching services designed to support knowledge development and implementation.

corwin.com/pd

>>> **PROFESSIONAL DEVELOPMENT RESOURCE CENTER**

The PD Resource Center provides school and district PD facilitators with the tools and resources needed to deliver effective PD.

corwin.com/pdrc

ONLINE >>> **ADVANCE**

Designed for K–12 teachers, Advance offers a range of online learning options that can qualify for graduate-level credit and apply toward license renewal.

corwin.com/advance

Contact a PD Advisor at (800) 831-6640 or visit www.corwin.com for more information